Get Wise! Mastering Reading Comprehension Skills

Get Wise!™

MASTERING Reading COMPREHENSION SKILLS

Nathan Barber

THOMSON
PETERSON'S

Australia • Canada • Mexico • Singapore • Spain • United Kingdom • United States

THOMSON

PETERSON'S

About Thomson Peterson's

Thomson Peterson's (www.petersons.com) is a leading provider of education information and advice, with books and online resources focusing on education search, test preparation, and financial aid. Its Web site offers searchable databases and interactive tools for contacting educational institutions, online practice tests and instruction, and planning tools for securing financial aid. Thomson Peterson's serves 110 million education consumers annually.

For more information, contact Thomson Peterson's, 2000 Lenox Drive, Lawrenceville, NJ 08648; 800-338-3282; or find us on the World Wide Web at www.petersons.com/about.

Production Editor: Alysha Bullock
Page Designer: Linda Williams
Illustrations: Gary Van Dzura

ISBN: 0-7689-1248-2

Printed in Canada

10 9 8 7 6 5 4 3 2 05 04

First Edition

Acknowledgments

Thanks to Christy and Noah for allowing me to hang out with the laptop more than with them during this project. See you soon!

Also, thanks to a great editor, Wallie Walker-Hammond, for the great insights.

Finally, a little shout-out to my second grade reading teacher who didn't put me in the star reading group: I bet you never imagined I'd actually grow up and write a reading book! Grin.

—Nathan Barber

Contents

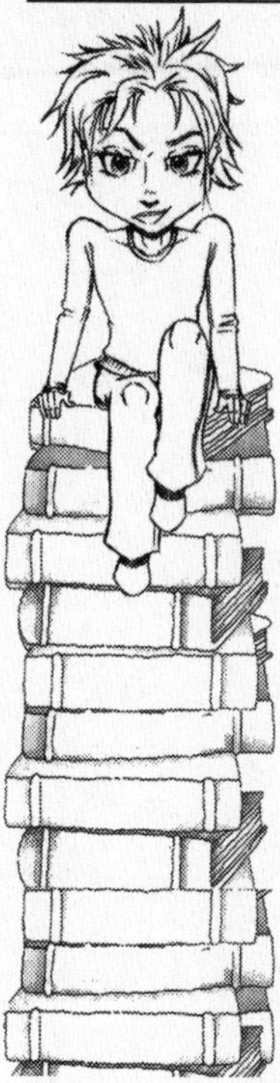

introduction

So, you need to learn how to read and comprehend. And you may think that you already know how, and you're not too excited about it.

You know, I'm a pretty good reader. The last book I read had only two or three pictures per page!

OK, Chi, I'm not sure if *Teen People* is required reading in any high school we know, but, contrary to popular opinion, reading is pretty cool. Some people like to read novels, some people like to read the sports section of the newspaper, and others like to read the back of the cereal box.

My dad gets real excited when my mom's new *Good Housekeeping* comes in the mail. But don't tell anybody. He'd be sooo embarrassed if anybody else knew.

Maybe you like to read, but it takes you forever to get through a couple of pages. Maybe you want to read more often, but you have a hard time remembering what you read, so you just don't bother anymore. Maybe you just don't like to read! Guess what? If any of these descriptions sound like you, you're not alone.

BUT, if you love to read, you'll love this book. If you don't, you're probably thinking: "What the heck have I gotten myself into?" Well, don't sweat it. This book is different from any other book you've ever read. "How?" you ask. Let us count the ways:

1. This is not your parent's reading book. There will be no "See Spot run" in this book.
2. There will be no dry, boring reading passages about white, fluffy clouds gently floating over lush, green pastures that are dotted with dainty, purple, and gold flowers, yada yada yada. None of that! (We didn't hire some guy with a dozen graduate degrees to give you a bunch of educational mumbo jumbo.)

Hey, I heard they didn't have enough in the budget to get a guy like that anyway!

3. At the end of each chapter, we'll give you the chance to find out how much you've learned.

A *chance* to find out how much we've learned? Oh, gee, thanks.

So, here's the plan. There are a few things that everyone can do to improve their reading skills. We'll show you those things and help you become a better reader. That's a good thing. Maybe you're wondering what it means "to be a better reader." Well, this book will help you become a better reader by helping you to understand what you read, remember the facts and important information in what you read, read faster, and much more. The good news is that you won't have to spend all day every day reading to be a better reader. Just a few minutes a day is all you need. Fair enough? Good. Let's go.

Any chance we could skip the book and just watch the movie instead?

chapter 1

A Wise Reader Knows *How* to Read

Think about this for a minute. Your teachers taught you how to read, to write, and do math when you started school in the first grade. Every year since then, your teachers have been adding to the skills you started learning when you were 6 years old. However, with each memorable year that passed, your teachers focused less and less on which skill? **Reading!** At some point, they just assumed you knew how to read and they stopped emphasizing reading skills. We're going to show you how to improve your reading skills by showing you how to become an *active* reader. When you actively read, you're engaging yourself with what you're reading, both mentally and physically (and no, this doesn't mean you should throw this book when you're finished!).

My friends and I are always active when we're reading each other's e-mail. My girl, Alysha, text messages me during her soccer games!

That's a pretty good trick, Chi, but that's not quite what we meant. Now, before you get any deeper into this book, and we know you're just dying to get deeper into this book, let's take a look at what it is you're reading and why you're reading it. Unless you're a total geek or you're this author's mom, you're reading this book for an educational purpose, right? Of course you are. There's a time and a place for every type of reading that you do. Are you that cereal-box reader? Then you can do that reading early in the morning when you're eating your bowl of cereal. Have you ever gotten a note from a friend? You can read that pretty much anywhere—on the bus, in the halls at school, at home on your bed with the TV or CD player going. But right now, you're reading a book to learn something. You are trying to learn something, right? Good.

Now, look around. Where are you right now? Ideally, you're in a quiet place with no distractions, such as a TV, telephone, boyfriend or girlfriend, bratty little brother. How's the lighting? The best lighting is not so bright that there's a glare on the page yet not so dark that you have to squint to see the words. Where are you sitting? Are you lying on your bed with your feet up? Are you outside nestled into a comfortable hammock? Are you in a hard, wooden chair with a straight back? Hopefully, if you answered "yes" to any of these, you'll be able to finish this chapter, but I wouldn't try *War and Peace* in any of those places. The best place to read something important, in other words, something you have to *remember*, is in a comfortable place but not a place that's so comfortable that you'll fall asleep. You should be able to sit comfortably so your back or neck won't ache and distract you.

There is something else you must understand before you can really understand how to read: *when* you read is just as important as *where* you read. If you have to read your science textbook to study for a test, you probably shouldn't do your reading 5 minutes before the test. You'll have to read so quickly that you're likely to miss or forget the important information. Likewise, you shouldn't read the textbook after you get home from a 10 P.M. movie. You'll be so tired that you won't be able to concentrate and remember the important information. In addition, you might even *fall asleep* while you're trying to read!

Well, you certainly won't remember the information that way, unless you fall asleep face down in your book and the process of osmosis transfers the information straight to your brain.

Have you ever tried to read something important after you had an argument with a parent or a friend or your boyfriend or girlfriend? That won't work too well, either, because you probably won't be able to concentrate and focus. If you really want to remember what you read, pick a time when you are awake, alert, and free from distractions. Pick a time when you have an adequate amount of time to complete your reading. If you need 45 minutes to read the reading selection, you need 45 consecutive, uninterrupted minutes of quiet time. Three 15-minute blocks of time spread out over an evening will not have the same effect as one 45-minute block of time.

I do my best reading at school during study hall. That way, I can go to the mall as soon as I get home.

Well, Chi, that's not a bad idea, but make sure that if you do your reading at school, you aren't distracted by the hot guy two rows over or by the guy sleeping and drooling on his desk. Sometimes it can be really hard to concentrate in a setting such as study hall, especially if your friends are trying to talk to you or pass you notes.

Now that you have a better idea about where and when to read, let's talk about your tools of the trade. What equipment do you need to be a better reader?

Uh … I do my best reading with a book!

Very funny, Chi. Seriously, though, besides just picking up your book, you may want to grab a few items to help you with your reading. Let's look at a short list, and then we'll examine each item more closely to figure why the heck we need it. Here's the list of "tools" you'll probably want to use:

★ Pencil, pen, or highlighter

★ Ruler or straightedge

★ Notebook

★ Dictionary

★ Flashlight

Before you get back into the reading, take a few moments and round these up. We'll see you back here in a few minutes.

OK, I have the stuff you wanted. I also grabbed a candy bar and a drink, just in case we're here for a while.

Great! Now that you have all your supplies, let's figure out what to do with each one of them.

First, you can use your "writing utensil," just a fancy way of saying **pen** or **pencil**, for following along under the lines in the book. It may help you focus on each word as you read. You can also use your pen or pencil to make notes in the margin, to circle or underline important words and phrases, or to make notes in your notebook. Just remember not to stick the pencil in your nose or in your ear; the Surgeon General has declared that this type of activity may be hazardous to your health.

Second, use your ruler or straightedge (instead of your pencil, if you wish) to follow each line of the book. Place it under the top line and then slide it down the page one line at a time as you read. This will help you focus on each word and will keep you from skipping lines as you read. Try not to use the ruler to rap across your little brother's knuckles when he tries to take this book away from you.

Third, use your notebook as a place to record important facts, names, definitions, and so on. Pretty much common sense, right?

Last is the flashlight. Always keep a flashlight handy, because if you are reading this book and the power goes out, you'll need a way to finish your reading.

There are several little pointers to remember as you read this and other books. **Don't rush through the reading.** Take your time, because you aren't in a race. We'll teach you how to increase your reading speed later. **Don't look ahead in the book.** Sometimes readers get frustrated when they look ahead and say to themselves, "Man, I still have 120 pages left to read." Don't worry about that, because you'll be reading small, manageable chunks and not 100 pages at a time. **Finally, try to enjoy reading.** Of course, you'll enjoy some readings more than others, but reading shouldn't be a chore. Have fun with your reading. You just might like it!

chapter 2

Just the Facts, Ma'am

A long, long time ago, back before any of you were even born, there was a police show on TV called *Dragnet.* (Yeah, we know it's back, but it's just not the same. Bear with us, please.) There was a character on the show who would interview witnesses and other people who were important to the case. Whenever the witnesses starting rambling, he would say, "Just the facts." He knew that out of all the words coming out of the witnesses' mouths, only some of them were important. Reading a passage out of a book, reading an article, or reading a story can be a lot like one of those interviews. You, the reader, have to weed out all the useless stuff and find the good stuff. Usually, it will be the hard facts.

There are several ways to find the important information in a reading passage. If you're lucky, the author of the book or whatever it is that you're reading will be really nice and put things in bold letters. It might look something like this:

> One of the first steps in creating a new nation is to create a **constitution**, or a written plan of government.

Now, if that sentence were in the middle of a paragraph, you could find it easily, and you could be darn sure that the bold information is important. After all, that's why the publisher spent the extra money on extra ink to print it in bold. But there are other ways to find important information. Bold words are good clues, but sometimes publishers put items in *italics* and sometimes publishers underline important things, too. Remember those tools we talked about in the last chapter? When you find these in a reading passage, pull a pen, pencil, or highlighter out of your pocket protector and put your tool to work. Either write the info in a notebook or go over it with a highlighter. Writing it out may help the information stick in your brain a little better, but highlighting is OK, too.

So what's the big deal? Just read and look for the bold, italicized, and underlined info—that's all it takes? Cool. But, hey, you could have told us that right off. Why do we need to go through the rest of this book? I think some authors like to stretch their ideas and get those big bucks for writing a bogus book!

Well, not really, Chi. Not every textbook will use these methods. Besides, if you get a letter from your significant other, it probably won't look like this:

> Hey, baby. I really **miss** you. I've been thinking about *you* all day. What are your plans for **Friday night**? Would you like to go see a *movie* or would you rather hang at the mall? **Don't call me** tonight because I'm grounded, but you can *e-mail* me. Peace out!

Do you see the point? An article, a memo, a story, or some other reading passage won't have things highlighted for you. So, how do you figure out what the most important information is in a passage if it doesn't jump off the page at you? There are a few ways to tell when something is really important. First, the most important information is usually mentioned first. The next most important information is second, and so on. The only exception is pretty obvious, because it might say something like, "And finally, the most important yada yada yada." Makes sense, doesn't it? Another clue about what is important is when a sentence is repeated or reworded. Another clue as to what is important is when a sentence is reworded or repeated.

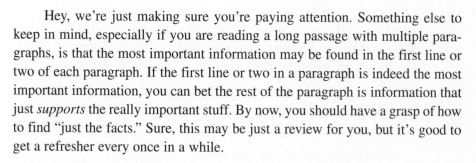

Oh, I get it. You said that last sentence twice, didn't you? Ha ha, very funny!

Hey, we're just making sure you're paying attention. Something else to keep in mind, especially if you are reading a long passage with multiple paragraphs, is that the most important information may be found in the first line or two of each paragraph. If the first line or two in a paragraph is indeed the most important information, you can bet the rest of the paragraph is information that just *supports* the really important stuff. By now, you should have a grasp of how to find "just the facts." Sure, this may be just a review for you, but it's good to get a refresher every once in a while.

OK, time to put your know-how to the test. Read the following passage and then answer the questions that follow the passage using the clues we just provided you for weeding out the facts.

The following is an excerpt from *The Art of Making a Sandwich* by Luigi Scallopini.

> The sandwich has a long and distinguished history, too long to delve into here. The creation of a sandwich, because of its long and storied history, is a task that should be taken seriously and should be handled responsibly. Paramount to sandwich-making is the selection of the bread. Selecting the right bread for a sandwich can make all the difference in the world. For example, selecting rye bread for a grilled cheese sandwich or selecting sourdough bread for chicken salad would be disastrous, an absolute calamity. On the other hand,

white bread with no crust would make a heavenly peanut butter and jelly sandwich.

Placement of sandwich condiments is also crucial. Mayonnaise must always be spread generously on the top slice of bread and mustard must always be spread on the bottom slice. The same rule applies to other condiments—complementing condiments must be spread on opposite slices and never on the same slice.

Furthermore, dressings, such as lettuce, tomatoes, pickles, onions, and cheese, must be either on one side of the meat or on the other, unless, of course, the sandwich is a vegetarian sandwich. Distribution of meat *must* be handled carefully and in such a manner that the amount of meat on the sandwich is neither overwhelming nor understated—not too much meat yet not too little.

1. Which of the following is the most important aspect of sandwich construction?

(A) Choice of bread

(B) Distribution of condiments

(C) Location of condiments

(D) Selection of sandwich dressings

2. Which of the following is the *second* most important aspect of sandwich construction?

(A) Spreading mayonnaise and mustard

(B) Placement of condiments

(C) Amount of meat

(D) Location of cheese

Oooh, my mom makes the *best* sandwiches for my lunch. They look so good, the sandwich lady in my school's cafeteria is always checking them out!

Hold on a few more minutes, Chi. We're getting close. Let's see how you did. For the first question, you probably noticed that we gave you a few hints. Because the information is listed first and because it is underlined, the most important aspect of sandwich making, according to Luigi, of course, is **(A)**, Choice of bread. For the second question, the hint was a little subtle, but it was still there. If you noticed the sentence with the italicized word, then you probably picked up on how important it is to place just the right amount of meat on a sandwich. If you picked up on that, you probably chose the correct answer, **(C),** Amount of meat.

Time for one more practice, and we'll be done for now. Just for you, Chi, we'll see if we can help you with the whole hunger issue so you can concentrate and make it through the exercise. Just like before, read the following paragraph and answer the questions that follow.

> Humans, like most other warm-blooded animals, have several peculiar bodily functions. One that is the most common in both humans and in animals, not to mention the most socially acceptable, is the sneeze. There are a few things that the public should know about the sneeze. First and foremost, when possible, the sneezer should cover his or her nose and mouth. The matter that is discharged from the nose and mouth during the sneeze travels at speeds of up to 60 miles per hour! Additionally, that sneeze may contain germs that could be passed along to innocent bystanders. People usually chuckle when someone sneezes because they think it's funny, but it's *not*.

1. The most crucial information the author wants to convey to the public about a sneeze is which of the following?

(A) It travels at a high velocity.

(B) It could carry germs.

(C) It is always loud.

(D) It is clean.

2. The most important thing to remember about sneezing is which of the following?

(A) It's important to cover one's nose and mouth during the sneeze.

(B) It's important to stand clear of sneezing bystanders.

(C) Sneezing is socially acceptable.

(D) Sneezing isn't funny.

Did that passage blow you away or what? Well, let's see how you did with no really obvious clues. Did you notice that the author said that the sneeze "may contain germs that could be passed along to an innocent bystander"? If you did, then you surely chose the correct answer, **(B)**, It could carry germs. As for the second question, you should have picked up on the clue of "first and foremost." If you noticed that, then you undoubtedly chose **(A)**, It is important to cover one's nose and mouth during the sneeze.

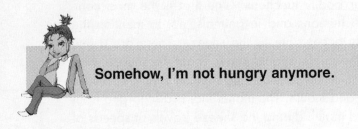

Somehow, I'm not hungry anymore.

OK, let's do a quick review.

Wise Note

Whenever you read a passage, the first thing to look for is the important information, you know, "just the facts." Weed out all the extra, unimportant information. The information may be in bold, *italics,* or <u>underlined</u> print. If it isn't, it may be at the beginning of the passage or at the beginning of paragraphs within the passage. Finally, the information may be repeated to emphasize its importance.

Got it? Excellent! You did great, and now we're ready to move on. See you in the next chapter.

chapter 3

The Hostess with the Mostest

OK, Chi, this one's for you. Well, maybe "mostest" isn't really a word, but you'll see where we're going with this in a minute. In the last chapter, we learned a few clues that can indicate which information within a passage is important. In this chapter, we focus on superlatives and absolutes.

Superlatives? What the heck are *latives,* and what makes them so *super*?

That's the **best** question you've asked in a while, Chi. If you have a question, you should **never** hesitate to ask. You're one of the **most** inquisitive people I have **ever** met—and I mean that in a good way, Chi. Are you starting to get the idea? Sometimes a writer uses literary tools called *superlatives* and *absolutes* to make a point or to stress importance. Superlatives are words that indicate extremes or the greatest (there's one) degree of something. Let's look at some examples of superlatives:

★ **Best**

★ **Worst**

★ **Most**

★ **Least**

★ **Biggest**

★ **Smallest**

★ **Hardest**

★ **Easiest**

In fact, superlatives are often used to indicate which information is crucial to a reading passage. Let's try a few of these and see what they might look like. You might read "the most homework," "the least important," "the hardest class," "the biggest loser," "the worst dressed," or "the best smile." Do you see how they show extremes? That's how the superlatives work. Maybe that qualifies reading as an extreme sport. What do you think, Chi?

Most definitely, not!

So, what are absolutes and how do they work? *Absolutes* are words that place limits and do not allow for exceptions. Let's take a look at a few examples of absolutes:

★ **Always**

★ **Never**

★ **All**

★ **None**

Now let's see what they might look like in a reading passage. You might read something like "all the cheerleaders," "none of the teachers," "always have bad breath," or "never take a shower." As with superlatives, absolutes can indicate important information. We could talk about this all day, but we should probably get you some practice. Ready to put this new knowledge to the test?

Absolutely!

Read the following passage, and keep an eye out for the **most** important information. (Did you get the hint?)

> Cheerleaders often do not get the respect they deserve. The general public often takes for granted the pure athleticism and brute strength required to perform the death-defying stunts. It should be noted that cheerleaders put their lives on the line every day, all in the name of duty and loyalty to school. There are several misconceptions about cheerleaders that discredit them as serious athletes. The application of makeup, for example, requires serious concentration, a steady hand, and incredible hand-eye coordination. The construction of the

spirit signs requires forethought and careful planning. The incredibly loud cheers that pierce the fans' ears require incredible diaphragm control and lung capacity. The most overlooked and underappreciated skill of cheerleaders, though, is the ability to loft pom-poms into the air on average 3,400 times per football game and 2,600 times per basketball game; those totals don't even include the 1,350 times at each pep rally that the cheerleaders raise their pom-poms proudly.

There is quite a bit of information in that passage, but, according to the author, one bit of information is more important and significant than any other. Did you find it? The sentence containing the superlative also contains the really important information. According to the author, the fact that people don't respect the pom-pom pumping power of cheerleaders is the "**most** overlooked and underappreciated" skills of cheerleaders. The author went on to supply more information about that fact, further demonstrating the importance of that piece of information. See how that works?

Give me a "y," give me an "e," give me an "s"!

Clever, Chi, very clever. Let's raise the stakes a bit and make things a tad more difficult. We'll make the passage a little longer and add a lot more information. Remember those reading tools—the pencil, highlighter, ruler, and so on? You may want to grab those and either circle or underline important information when you see it. Just remember that what we are looking for is the **most** important information and not all the information. Got it? Got your tools?

Busy teens on the go in today's fast-paced hectic world often do without when it comes to breakfast. However, it isn't good to skimp on breakfast. When there simply isn't time for a good, old-fashioned balanced, nutritional breakfast, such as bacon, eggs, toast, juice, milk, and sausage, there is another option: cereal. There are many good breakfast cereals on the market today, and some of them are even great breakfast cereals. Some cereals are full of nuts, berries, grains, and things that a horse might eat. Many cereals are fortified with enough iron, vitamins, and minerals to set off a metal detector. Some great cereals have trademark qualities, such as chocolate, cinnamon, peanut butter, or cookie chunks mixed right in. Some great cereals have frosting or some other mystery substance coating each and every tiny little piece. But what do the best cereals have in common? All the best cereals have one thing in common: sugar and lots of it. Whether the sugar is baked in or sprinkled on the outside, sugar-packed cereal is the only way to go. Some great cereals have less sugar than others, but none of the best cereals is sugar-free. Today's busy teens need all the sugar that cereal can provide so they can make it through third and fourth periods to lunch. Granted, there are side effects of sugar-laden cereal, but the positives certainly outweigh the negatives. For example, sugary cereal can cause tooth decay if teeth aren't brushed regularly. Also, many cereals have preservatives that might do who-knows-what to your brain, but that hasn't really been proven yet. The most serious side effect of cereal, sugary cereal, that is, is the increased risk of hyper-behavior in first and second periods because of the sugar rush. All in all, cereal just can't be beat.

1. According to the passage, what is the significance of sugar in cereal?
   (A) Many good cereals have sugar.
   (B) Some great cereals have sugar.
   (C) All the best cereals have sugar.
   (D) None of the best cereals have sugar.

2. Which of the following is the most serious negative side effect of the best cereals?

   (A) Tooth decay

   (B) Hyperactivity for a few hours after eating

   (C) Lethargy

   (D) Malnutrition

Well, let's see how you did with the longer, more detailed, and complicated passage. For the first question, did you choose **(C),** All the best cereals have sugar? Good! Obviously, the author was hyped up on sugar when he wrote this, but he made sure to use a superlative, "best," and an absolute, "all," in the same sentence to show importance and significance. Let's look at the second question. Did you find the superlative "worst?" If you did, then you most probably chose the correct answer, **(B),** Hyperactivity for a few hours after eating. It's as simple as that. Did you use your "writing utensil" to circle or underline? It helped, didn't it?

Great! Let's do a quick review before we move on to a new chapter and a new skill.

Wise Note

When looking for the most important information in a passage, look for superlatives and absolutes. These are words such as *best*, *worst*, *biggest*, and *smallest* or words such as *all* and *none*. Writers use superlatives and absolutes to show importance and significance.

And that is why, Chi, we say that you *absolutely* are the hostess with the mostest!

Hey, I'm all that and a bag of chips! Who knew?

chapter 4

Total Recall

You know, the human brain is unbelievable. It can hold as much information as you can stuff into it. Well, *most* people's brains are like that. There is, of course, the occasional person whose brain reaches maximum density at some point and then loses a fact or piece of information for every new fact that gets put in there. The brain is like a sponge. No, not soft, wet, and squishy. Absorbent. So, now you know that your brain can hold more information than you can put into it in a lifetime. That, of course, begs the question: "Why can't I remember the answers on the literature test I studied for last night?" It isn't because you can't remember, and it isn't even because your teacher's sole purpose in life is to make you squirm. One of the biggest reasons that perhaps you, along with zillions of other students around the world, don't always remember things that you read is your *approach* to reading.

Are you telling me you can't read something and just know it right away?

Sure, Chi, you can if you have a photographic memory. In fact, more people than you might think actually do have a photographic memory. But, if you're not one of those people, you'll need a plan of attack. Believe it or not, you've already been practicing a little for this chapter. Remember all those tools we talked about? Well, you'll need them from here on out. You definitely will need a "writing utensil" of some sort, even if it's a crayon or eyeliner. You may want to grab a notebook, too.

Earlier, we talked about circling and underlining important information. We do that to *locate* the information. What you may not realize is that this actually helps the brain to absorb that information. The best way to remember information is to *rewrite* it. Back in their day, your parents and grandparents took classes in spelling, and their teachers made them write spelling words over and over and over again. If you have the time to take notes on what you read, that's the way to go. However, if you're reading a passage on a class examination or on a standardized test at school, you know the teacher or proctor won't give you extra time to take notes. Therefore, there has to be another way.

Let me guess. We're about to find out?

Actually, Chi, you already know how.

1. Slide your pencil or ruler along under the lines as you read, and you will tend to concentrate more and skip less.
2. Circle or underline, and you are doing the next best thing to rewriting the information.
3. Make notes in the margin, and you'll be able to quickly find the info you need to answer a question.

Let's do a little experiment. Put down your pencil and your ruler. Read the passage straight through, and see if you can answer the questions that follow.

Peter and Paul had the directions that their friend Barry gave them, but they weren't sure exactly how to get to

McMillan's. The two guys stopped and asked an older fellow at a gas station called Phil's Fill-It-Up. The old guy, whose name was Perry, said McMillan's was located at the corner of Broad Parkway and Park Road. Peter and Paul thought they understood the directions, so they hopped in their car and took off. As they drove down Park Road, they saw McMillan's ahead on the left, just past the intersection of Broad Parkway. The two hungry guys then faced a dilemma. Should they drive down Park Road and park in the driveway, or should they turn and drive down Broad Parkway and park on the road? Peter and Paul decided to park on the road, just past the driveway on Park Road so they could just drive away after they finished their meal.

Uh, yawn ... what did I just read? Anybody else a little lost?

OK, here are your questions. Try to answer them without referring back to the passage.

* First, what two people gave directions?
* Second, on which street was the driveway located?

Well, can you answer them? Probably, not. OK, let's try this again, but we're going to take a little different approach this time. This time, use your pencil or pen to underline, circle, make notes, draw arrows, or whatever you need to do to keep everything straight in your mind. Got your pencil? Let's go.

Peter and Paul had the directions, given to them by their friend Barry, but they weren't sure exactly how to get to McMillan's. The two guys stopped and asked an older fellow at a gas station called Phil's Fill-It-Up. The old guy, whose name was Perry, said McMillan's was located at the corner of Broad Parkway and Park Road. Peter and Paul thought they understood the directions, so they hopped in their car and took off. As they drove down Park Road, they saw McMillan's ahead on the left, just past the intersection of Broad Parkway. The two hungry guys then faced a dilemma. Should they drive down Park Road and park in the driveway, or should they turn and drive down Broad Parkway and park on the road? Peter and Paul decided to park on the road, just past the driveway on Park Road so they could just drive away after they finished their meal.

OK, let's answer those questions again.

★ First, what two people gave directions? Barry and Perry gave the directions–Barry originally and then Perry at the gas station.

★ Second, on which street was the driveway located? The driveway was on Park Road.

I think they should've just gone somewhere else to eat.

Did you get them? Did the circling, and so on, help? Excellent. Just remember that names, dates, and places are always good things to remember. Of course, if you find something in **bold**, *italics,* or underlining, then you may want to circle or make a note of that. Maybe you're reading a passage that contains instructions or directions. You may want to circle or underline each step. Let's do another one and let you practice a little more.

Get Wise!

Read the following passage and answer the questions that follow.

> The substitute teacher who filled in for Mr. Barton yesterday didn't do such a great job. For starters, she showed up at 8:15, but the first class began at 8:05. Mr. Barton left instructions for her on his desk, but apparently, she had some difficulty reading his handwriting. The sub made the first class stand up, get in line in order of oldest to youngest, and then sit back down in that order. Then the sub changed her mind and arranged everyone in boy-girl-boy-girl order. When everybody settled down, the sub wrote the assignment on the board. The assignment was to write an essay on whether or not aliens exist. Right before everyone started the assignment, however, she introduced herself to the class. Her name was Mary Lou Baloo. Mrs. Baloo told the class that she was not really a substitute teacher but that she was a secret agent working undercover for the government, but she had worked as a teacher before. She also said that she had worked as a ballet dancer, a construction worker, a librarian, a chimney sweep, and as an editor for a major publishing company. She then whispered that she was investigating and observing one of the other teachers in the school because that teacher was suspected of being an alien. Of course, the class kind of chuckled and assumed she was kidding. Mrs. Baloo went on to say that she was originally from Kansas and her maiden name was Brown. She said the government recruited her and moved her to Thailand, then to Kenya, then to Guinea, then to Monaco, then to Albania, and then back to the United States. She met her husband, Hulla, in Guinea. Strangely enough, they became Mr. and Mrs. Hulla Baloo. About the time she finished her story, two

men in white suits entered the class, grabbed Mrs. Baloo, and dragged her away. Nobody has neither seen nor heard from her since.

1. Which of the following countries had Mrs. Baloo never visited while in the government service?

(A) Taiwan
(B) Albania
(C) Kenya
(D) Thailand

2. In what order were the students seated when Mrs. Baloo began her story?

(A) Alphabetical
(B) Boy-girl
(C) Oldest to youngest
(D) Youngest to oldest

3. What was Mrs. Baloo's maiden name?

(A) Green
(B) White
(C) Brown
(D) Barton

4. Which of the following jobs had Mrs. Baloo never held?

(A) Ballet dancer
(B) Court reporter
(C) Construction worker
(D) Teacher

How Wise?

1. (A) Taiwan

2. (B) boy-girl

3. (C) Brown

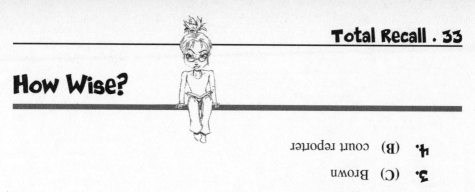

4. (B) court reporter

So, hopefully, your reading passage has circles and lines written everywhere with notes in the margin as well. The whole point of this chapter is to get you used to this method of memory recall. Let's do one final quick review of the strategies in this chapter, and then we'll be done.

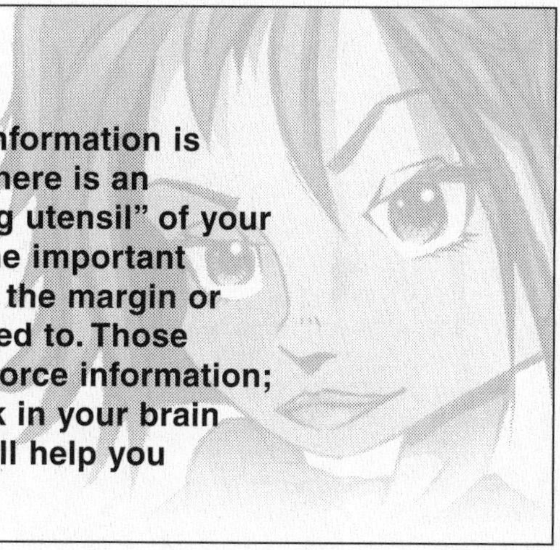

Wise Note

Remember that rewriting information is best, but when you can't, there is an alternative. Use the "writing utensil" of your choice to circle or underline important information. Make notes in the margin or draw arrows, too, if you need to. Those techniques all help to reinforce information; in other words, things stick in your brain better. These little tricks will help you recall facts.

Oooh! I think my brain is getting full! I hope information doesn't start oozing out of my ears! Especially 'cause it's not so pretty.

chapter 5

What *Are* You Reading?

Let's face it, you don't read your biology textbook the same way that you read your e-mail. And you won't have to plow through a novel the same way you would through a U.S. history textbook. If you're reading a sports or fashion magazine, you don't have to pull all the facts out of the text. Same thing with a newspaper article. However, if you are reading a passage on a standardized test, you'll need to remember everything, or at least *a lot*.

My mom remembers the lyrics to all of the Led Zeppelin records. She must have one of those *phonographic* memories you were talking about before.

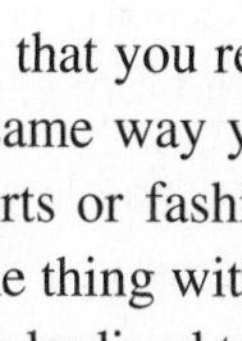

That was *photographic* memory, Chi. There's a way to read different things, and it's pretty important that you know:

- ★ What you're reading
- ★ Why you're reading it
- ★ How much info you're going to need

Let's start with the hard-core academic stuff. Subjects like biology, math, grammar, history, and others require that you glean as much information as possible from the text. Also, reading passages on standardized tests require that you remember a great deal of information and facts. To do all of this, you've got to *slow down* and *use your writing stick to highlight the important information.* Chances are that the information you highlight is going to be tested.

You'll be able to go through the next group of readings a little more quickly, but not too fast. As we said, if, for example, you're reading a memo from your boss about being on time or a newspaper article about Michael Jordan's last game or the latest Orson Scott Card novel, you don't have to have every little fact and detail committed to memory. When you're reading these kinds of texts, you really need only the general idea of the passage, along with a few details. Obviously, if you're going to be tested on the reading, make sure you read a little more carefully.

The last group of readings can be done as quickly as you would like, as long as you are doing more than just highlighting words or "word calling." In other words, *don't just read the words*. Read it, and *understand* what you're reading. You can read things such as e-mails, letters, fiction, and casual reading that you're doing for fun and enjoyment. If the fiction is full of action scenes or lots of back-and-forth dialogue, you can move through it quickly. Let's face it, you won't be tested on these things, and you won't have to absorb all the information in these selections, either. Just relax and enjoy these, but read them as quickly as you would like.

Reading for *fun*? Is this a trick?

No, Chi, reading for fun is not a trick, but let's do a little exercise to get you used to thinking in these terms. At the beginning of each of the following brief excerpts you will see two blanks. In the first blank, write what type of reading passage it is.

★ Textbook

★ Newspaper

★ Personal e-mail

★ Letter

★ Memo

★ Novel

You get the idea. In the second blank, write "slowly," "medium," or "quickly" according to the speed at which you should read that type of passage. Look at the following example:

textbook ____ slowly

The layer of our atmosphere that protects the earth from many harmful rays given off by the sun is called the **ozone layer**. Chlorofluorocarbons from aerosol cans damage the ozone layer.

Let's give it a try.

Get Wise!

In the first blank, write what type of reading passage it is. And in the second blank, write "slowly," "medium," or "quickly" based on the speed at which you should read that type of passage.

1. ________________ ________________

Yo, Amy said J.J. was putting the moves on Missy at lunch today. Write back ASAP.

2. ________________ ________________

Mayor Sealy's office refused to answer questions yesterday, although sources have reported that the mayor will indeed retire at the end of his term.

3. ________________ ________________

The Founding Fathers based much of their political philosophy on the writings of John Locke. Locke's most influential idea was that of natural rights, or life, liberty and property.

4. ________________ ________________

All personnel should return to business attire for the remainder of the fiscal year. Summer/casual attire is discouraged until next May.

5. ________________ ________________

The samurai drew his sword and faced his opponent. The samurai's opponent, likewise, drew his sword and walked slowly toward his foe. In the blink of an eye, the two mighty warriors found themselves engaged in a fight to the death.

6. __________________ __________________

I look forward to seeing you at Christmas. Hopefully you can arrange for your extended family to stay in town, too, so that we can all have a holiday together.

7. __________________ __________________

The VHS Vikings out-rebounded their opponent 34–26 and outscored the Warriors 12–5 in the last 2 minutes of the game to emerge as the District champions. Noah Jordan led all scorers, with 23 points in the 56–51 win.

8. __________________ __________________

The two looked deeply into one another's eyes and hoped that the moment would last forever. They knew, though, that in a few moments, Tom would climb aboard the train and they might never see each other again.

9. __________________ __________________

According to the Constitution, to be eligible to be the President of the United States of America, a person must be a natural-born citizen, at least 35 years of age, and have been a resident of the United States for at least fourteen years.

10. __________________ __________________

The cyclic exchange of respiratory gases within an organism is known as respiration. Cellular respiration involves the production of ATP molecules within the mitochondria; oxygen is used, and carbon dioxide is produced.

Wow! I hadn't heard about J.J. and Missy at lunch. That's *so* not right. I wonder if Megan knows?

How Wise?

1. e-mail/letter, quickly
2. newspaper, medium
3. textbook, slowly
4. memo, medium
5. novel, medium
6. e-mail/letter, quickly
7. newspaper, medium
8. novel, medium
9. textbook, slowly
10. textbook, slowly

There is a big difference between reading a textbook and reading an article and between a novel and an e-mail. That's why it is so important to know what you're reading and why you're reading it! See you in the next chapter!

Puzzle 1

Complete the following puzzle using the words you just learned in Chapters 1–5. Puzzle solutions are in the back of the book.

Across

1. WORDS SUCH AS *ALWAYS*, *NEVER*, *ALL*, *NONE*

5. TOOL FOR HELP WITH DIFFICULT WORDS

7. ANOTHER WAY A PUBLISHER PRINTS IMPORTANT INFORMATION

8. FOR JOTTING NOTES IN WHILE READING

10. WAY TO EMPHASIZE IMPORTANT INFO; WAY TO EMPHASIZE IMPORTANT INFO

13. YET ANOTHER WAY A PUBLISHER PRINTS IMPORTANT INFORMATION

14. ELECTRONIC READING MATERIAL THAT ALLOWS FOR FAST READING AND LOW COMPREHENSION

Down

2. WORDS SUCH AS *BEST*, *WORST*, *GREATEST*, *MOST*

3. REQUIRES THE SLOWEST READING AND MOST COMPREHENSION

4. FUNNY NAME FOR PEN, PENCIL, ETC.

5. READING ENVIRONMENT SHOULD BE FREE OF THESE

6. ONE OF THE TOOLS NEEDED TO BE A BETTER READER

9. ALLOWS FOR FASTEST READING AND LEAST COMPREHENSION

11. REQUIRES MEDIUM READING SPEED AND MEDIUM COMPREHENSION

12. ONE WAY A PUBLISHER PRINTS IMPORTANT INFORMATION

Comprendé?

You now have the tools to pick out the important information in a reading passage, but that is only the tip of the iceberg. After all, there is more to reading than just picking out facts and remembering those facts. How boring would it be if names and places were the only things you actually got out of a story? How tough would it be to take a junior- or senior-level literature class and the most you got out of it was a huge list of main characters, place settings, and so on? You have to have the facts, but you also have to be able to grasp concepts and see the bigger picture. That's all part of what is called **reading comprehension**. Comprehension goes deeper than just remembering. Comprehension includes understanding the main idea that an author is trying to convey. Comprehension includes realizing and understanding where a reading passage is going and from what point of view it is coming. Comprehension involves the ability to distinguish between fact and opinion. Comprehension is what we're working toward with this book. Comprendé?

OK, time for me to insert myself. So, what is *comprehension*? In other words:

- ★ **I'm down with that.**
- ★ **I hear ya.**
- ★ **True dat!**
- ★ **Rockin'!**

All right, thanks, maybe. We'll just move on here. In the next several chapters, we're going to work on:

- ★ Identifying the main idea
- ★ Determining the point of view
- ★ Predicting what will happen next

No matter what you're reading—a short story, a letter from your school, even an e-mail from your friend—you must figure out what it's all about. One of the most common complaints we hear from students is, "I just don't get it."

Uh ... are those students referring to the reading passage?

Well, yeah, but the point is ...

No, that's *my* point.

Now *we* don't know what the point is. Perhaps Chi is demonstrating how distractions can lead you astray? Oh, right, my point was … (am I safe, now?) that not all ideas are stated directly. In fact, in many works of fiction, the main idea is often *un*stated, so you need to work through all the details to figure it out. But there is a *way* to do this that is not often obvious. And that's why you have this book. We're going to provide you with some great tips and strategies that will make reading not only easier but also more enjoyable. Here are some tips you can start out with for the next few chapters:

★ As you work through the next chapters, don't just read the words, *think* about the words. Try to visualize what you're reading and imagine the events in your head. Have you ever just read something, and suddenly, you have no idea what you just read? That's because your brain is not *engaged*. Imagining will engage you.

★ Try to find a good speed for your reading. If you find that you are flying through the passages, then *slow down*—try to absorb the information as you go. Don't be afraid to stop reading for a moment just to think about what you just read. After a paragraph, pause for a moment and think; picture it in your head and *then* move on. This way, you won't have to always read something two or three times to get it.

Keep using the tips from the previous chapters to help you identify and recall information. You will continue to build your reading skills, one by one. Oh, yes, one more piece of advice: Enjoy it, and have fun!

Hey, I'm always up for fun. Should I bring my chips and dip?

In the next several chapters, we're going to work on things such as finding the main idea, reading between the lines, determining point of view, figuring out an author's point of view, predicting what will happen next in a passage, and more. Remember we said reading can be cool? We have to be able to prove that, and we're pretty sure that reading just to recall facts and figures is not cool. If that were all you wanted out of a reading experience, you would just read a dictionary or, if you are a little more adventurous, perhaps an encyclopedia.

Now we're talking! When I read, sometimes I just don't get it.

chapter 7
What's the Big Idea?

It doesn't matter what you're reading—a story, a letter from your friend, a passage on a reading comprehension test—the first thing you should ask yourself is *What is this about?* In other words, what is the writer's **main idea**? The main idea is the central point or idea that the writer wants you to understand. That's what we're going to focus on for a while. In the next several chapters, we'll guide you through finding the main idea in several different types of reading passages. We'll also show you how to understand *implied* main ideas, which are main ideas that are not stated but are strongly suggested.

So the main idea of this chapter is the main idea? I already know that. Maybe I could just get some more chips and dip.

Not so fast, Chi. There must be *something* you can learn from the rest of the chapter. Just hang in there; it won't take long. We'll break it down for you.

The first thing to remember is that the main idea of a paragraph or passage is simply *what the paragraph is about*. If the main idea is stated directly, it often appears in the first sentence of a paragraph or even the last sentence of a reading passage. Be careful, though, and try not to confuse the main idea with the *subject* of the paragraph. There's a difference between the subject and the main idea. Take a look at this passage:

> Once upon a time, there lived a witch. Because of the tricks she played on all of the children in the village, the witch was considered the meanest lady alive. The witch had been known to turn herself into a dog and then eat the children's homework. The witch would sneak into the children's rooms and unmake their beds after they left for school. The witch even stole all the Tooth Fairy's reward money once and left many of the children both toothless and bankrupt. The meanest trick she ever played on the children was on the first day of school last year. She taped dark paper over the children's bedroom windows, and they overslept! The entire fourth grade was 2 hours late for school on the first day. The children in the village thought she was even meaner than their English teacher.

Which of the following is the main idea of the previous passage?

(A) Once upon a time, there lived a witch.

(B) The witch was very mean.

(C) The witch didn't want children to have fun.

(D) The witch didn't like children to go to school.

(E) The witch's favorite snack was homework

I never liked that mean witch in *The Wizard of Oz*. What was her name? Oh, I can't remember which witch was which, East or West. Come to think of it, they were both pretty creepy!

But did you choose the correct answer, Chi? If you chose **(A)**, well, that's not right. This passage is *about* the witch, yes—but "the witch" is not the main idea of the passage. The witch is just the *subject* or *whom* the passage is about. The main idea has to say something *about* the witch. Remember that the main idea is the idea that holds the passage together. Read the passage again.

> Once upon a time, there lived a witch. Because of the tricks she played on all of the children in the village, the witch was considered the meanest lady alive. The witch had been known to turn herself into a dog and then eat the children's homework. The witch would sneak into the children's rooms and unmake their beds after they left for school. The witch even stole all the Tooth Fairy's reward money once and left many of the children both toothless and bankrupt. The meanest trick she ever played on the children was on the first day of school last year. She taped dark paper over the children's bedroom windows, and they overslept! The entire fourth grade was 2 hours late for school on the first day. The children in the village thought she was even meaner than their English teacher.

OK, already. I get it! The witch was MEAN!

Great, Chi. The main idea of the passage *is* that the witch was very mean. The first sentence isn't really a main idea, because it only tells you "There lived a witch." The rest of the sentences don't necessarily support that. However, the second sentence says the witch was mean, and the rest of the passage details how and why the witch was considered mean. If you think the first sentence is only the *subject*, check out the second sentence. That's probably it. Remember, though, there might be times when the main idea is found at the end of the passage and, as we mentioned (if you were paying attention), we'll cover that in the next chapter. So let's try another passage.

> Barney is an outstanding ice-cream salesman. Barney has sold more gallons of fudge-ripple by himself than most fleets of ice-cream trucks do in a year. Barney has been the top Dream Bar salesman six of the last seven years. Barney is such a good salesman that other ice-cream truck fleets send him their overstocks of pistachio-peanut butter swirl, and he sells *every* last cone. Barney even wrote a training manual on how to successfully persuade customers to buy Spunky Sprinkles and Sumptuous Sauces for their ice cream. Barney is the only ice-cream truck driver in the country who has been inducted in the Freezer of Fame before the age of 50. Perhaps the most remarkable fact of all is that Barney works in Anchorage, Alaska, yet he still manages to sell more ice cream than drivers in Phoenix, Dallas, Miami, and Orlando.

Which of the following is the main idea of this passage?

(A) Barney wrote a training manual for other salespeople.

(B) Barney is Cold Gold's all-time top-selling ice-cream salesperson.

(C) Barney sells more ice cream than any other ice-cream salesperson in the world.

(D) Barney lives and works in Alaska.

(E) Barney is wealthy.

Man, Barney this and Barney that. Have you guys ever heard of a *pronoun*?

Of course we have. But don't you just love that name, *Barney*? OK, back to the main idea. The correct answer is **(C)**, and if that's what you chose, then you got the main idea. This passage couldn't stop singing the praises of Barney. All of the sentences in the passage support that idea. In any well-written paragraph, the body of the paragraph will support the main idea. Now that you have the hang of it, let's try another.

Let's take a look at a newspaper article and see if we can locate the main idea. Sometimes newspaper articles don't flow exactly the same way that other reading passages do.

Newspaper? Who reads the newspaper? Except for my dumb brother, and now he's at Harvard.

Local Twins Celebrate 100th

Ida Belle and Uda Belle Smith, both of Central City, turned 100 years old on Friday. Ida Belle and Uda Belle, identical twins, are believed to be the world's oldest surviving twins.

When asked who was older, Ida Belle turned to Uda Belle and said, "I'm not sure, do you remember who's older?" Uda Belle replied, "I declare, Ida Belle, we were born on the same day. How can one of us be older than the other?"

> **The Smith twins, who proudly displayed their faded and crumbling baby pictures, couldn't remember which picture was which and who was who. That didn't dampen the spirits of the two centenarians, though.**
>
> **The two 100-year-old great-great-grammas celebrated their momentous day at the Shady Acres Retirement Home with a rambunctious game of BINGO with a few of their closest friends.**

Which of the following is the main idea of the previous passage?

(A) The Smith twins turned 100 years old.

(B) The Smith twins suffer from senile dementia.

(C) The Smith twins have retired after 100 years.

(D) The Smith twins are the oldest people in the retirement home.

(E) The Smith twins are local celebrities.

You gotta be kidding me! They played BINGO? You can bet that when I'm 100, I'll still be crackin' wise with these *Get Wise!* authors.

You're probably right, Chi. But did you figure out the answer to the question? The whole point of the newspaper article is to tell readers about the twins who just turned 100 years old (choice **A**). Sometimes the main idea in a newspaper article is easy to spot, and sometimes it is more difficult. We'll look at some more difficult passages in the next chapter.

OK, now do you get the idea? Well, let's try an exercise to finish this chapter. Read the following passages. You should notice that each passage is missing the main idea. You'll need to choose the sentence that best states the main idea of each passage and that should have been included in the passage.

Try not to peek at the answers until **after** you do the exercise!

Kinda hard to peek when the answers are UPSIDE DOWN!

Get Wise!

1. Sometimes, twenty screaming kids throwing birthday cake and ice cream can be rather overstimulating. Then there's always Aunt Lulu, who likes to squeeze everyone's cheeks and give them big disgusting kisses. After kisses, cake, and ice cream, there're the presents. All the other kids have to sit around and act like they're having fun while the spoiled birthday brat tears through the presents. Usually the brat's mother hovers over him and says, "Oh, what a wonderful idea for a present," while the kid ravages his stack of gifts. Then, when the birthday brat opens the last present, he inevitably says, "Aw, man, is that all?" Of course by the end of the party, everyone is tired and cranky. Someone has gotten sick from eating too much junk food. Someone else has gotten a black eye or a bloody nose because somebody accidentally invited the school bully. With all these hazards, it's no wonder that parents only subject kids to these once a year!

Which of the following sentences contains the main idea for the previous passage?

(A) Birthday parties are great fun.

(B) Birthday parties should be thrown more than once a year.

(C) A birthday party can be a traumatic event for a kid.

(D) Only kids enjoy birthday parties.

(E) Only adults enjoy birthday parties.

2. Many bands pulled crazy publicity stunts like free concerts on rooftops. Some bands adopted strange names, such as Spandau Ballet, Kajagoogoo, Twisted Sister, and A Flock of Seagulls. Other bands wore bizarre clothes, such as rubber or leather pants, shredded t-shirts, boots with 10-inch soles, and gaudy jewelry. Many bands wore makeup—tons of it. Perhaps the most memorable thing about the bands of the 1980s was their hair. Most of the bands had long, pretty hair like girls. Some had cans of hairspray and gobs of gel in their hair to make their hair stand up or frizz out from their heads. Some went with dyed hair to stand out from the crowd. Some bands made their mark with outlandish stage acts involving cages or even by flying around hooked to wires. Fortunately, or unfortunately, depending on your perspective, most of the bands of the 1980s were one-hit wonders whose musical careers were short lived.

Which of the following sentences contains the main idea for the previous passage?

(A) Rock bands from the 1980s are sorely missed.

(B) Rock bands from the 1980s were boring.

(C) Rock bands from the 1980s were great musicians.

(D) Rock bands from the 1980s often were rather outrageous.

(E) Rock bands from the 1980s are sure to make a comeback because of their wild styles.

How Wise?

1. **(C)** A birthday party can be a traumatic event for a kid.

2. **(D)** Rock bands from the 1980s often were rather outrageous.

chapter 8

OK, Wise Guy, *Now* Do You Get the Idea?

Finding the main idea is simple when you know *where* to look. If the main idea isn't located in the first sentence or two, you may have to use your detective skills to search for it. And, as any good detective knows, to get to the bottom of a mystery you have to look for clues:

- ★ You know that the main idea *sums up* the passage, and the other sentences in the passage support or back up the main idea.
- ★ The other sentences that surround the main idea may give details that further explain the main idea. Those details and facts will be the **clues** that will lead you to the main idea.

Follow these clues the way a detective would follow muddy footprints across white carpet, and you'll be on the right track. So let's put your gumshoe skills to the test.

You know, my mom has a fit when my little brother gets gum in his hair. She might not mind the gum on his shoe, though ... much easier to get off!

No, Chi, not gum on your shoe, *gumshoe*! A gumshoe is a … oh, never mind.

> It was a cold and rainy night, and the wind was blowing in under the door and around the windows. It seemed especially cold because the utility company shut off the gas—no more furnace. It was quiet that night, too. The phone didn't ring once. Nobody walked into the office. Nobody e-mailed. The stack of empty envelopes on the desk was made up mostly of bills and junk mail; there were no checks, though, and no cash payments. The Walker-Hammond Detective Agency went out of business and closed its doors. The out-of-work detectives traded in their badges and notepads for keyboards. The office sat empty and dark. The electricity, too, had gone unpaid for too long, so the electric company pulled the plug. The landlord hung an eviction notice on the door. In the corner, next to the old TV/VCR combo, sat a pile of *Scooby Doo* videos, obviously training videos for any new detectives. The training manuals, a dust-covered stack of *Scooby Doo* comics, lay strewn about the floor.

Hey, man, quit hatin' on Scooby!

Sorry, Chi. Did you find the main idea of the passage? We'll give you a clue: The main idea isn't at the beginning of the passage, but you probably know that already. Did you notice that most of the sentences are simply details that support one of the sentences? Did you also notice which of the sentences is supported by the others? If you did, then you followed the clues like a good sleuth and you unraveled the mystery. The main idea of the passage is "The Walker-Hammond Detective Agency went out of business and closed its doors." Notice that all of the surrounding sentences give evidence that, indeed, the agency had gone out of business. Nice going, Sherlock (or should we say, Scooby?).

Let's try another. Read the next the passage and uncover the mystery of the main idea.

> Students seeking admissions to the Considerable Cranium College Preparatory School (CCCPS) must pass a series of extensive examinations that measure everything from IQ to physical fitness. On admission to the school, students must attend a two-week orientation session in which they must memorize the periodic table of the elements, learn Greek and Latin, and memorize ARCO's *Master the SAT*. In the first week of school, which begins August 1, students are expected to choose a major, a minor, a specialty, a backup specialty, and a career track. Typical course loads include the obvious English, math, social studies, science, and fine arts. However, additional core courses include international diplomacy, political theory, sport pedagogy, and film history. Students who graduate from CCCPS often laugh at graduates of other high schools in the tri-state area when they talk about having survived on 2 hours of homework each night; it is common for CCCPS students to sleep for only 2 hours each night. In addition, CCCPS alumni turn up their noses at other high school graduates when they complain about not graduating until the first week of June; CCCPS graduation is typically held in the last week of July each year. The graduation rate at CCCPS, based on the number of students who enter each year as freshmen, averages approximately 50 percent. This means that half of the best and brightest from the tri-state area just aren't CCCPS material. The Considerable Cranium College Preparatory School is the most challenging and rigorous high school in the entire tri-state area.

Wait a minute! This morning, before I left for school, I saw a note on the refrigerator that said, "Call Ms. Barnett at CCCPS on Friday morning." Oh, no!

Looks like you have another reason to use your detective skills, Chi. But we digress. The previous passage is just a little longer than the first. That means that you had a few more clues to wade through to get to the main idea. The passage is so full of facts and figures that the only logical choice for the main idea is "The Considerable Cranium College Prep School is the most challenging and rigorous high school in the entire tri-state area." Look back at the passage and see how every other sentence presents a bit of evidence that proves or supports the main idea.

I definitely have the idea now!

So you've learned how to find the main idea of a reading passage no matter where the author has placed it in the text. Let's do a couple of practice passages for review, and then we'll move on to our next concept.

Get Wise!

Read the following passages, then answer the question that follows each.

1. Most areas of virgin, untapped, and undeveloped wilderness are natural habitats for several creatures. Beautiful birds, owls, and deer live in the wilderness. However, so do coyotes, bobcats, snakes, scorpions, ticks, ants, spiders, and other creepy-crawly critters. Tents, campfires, and wiener roasts, not to mention sleeping bags full of people, are not found naturally in the wilderness. These unnatural additions to a wilderness area can attract all sorts of curious critters. When critters cross paths with campers, especially inexperienced campers, mayhem is bound to occur. Camping in the wilderness can be a harrowing experience for people who are unfamiliar with the outdoors. Inexperienced campers may leave tents unzipped, thereby inviting unwanted guests, such as mosquitoes, scorpions, ants, spiders, and snakes, into the tents. Rookie campers may leave food out overnight, thus attracting hordes of hungry wildlife, including bears. First-time campers may forget things, such as insect repellent, extra matches, and toilet tissue, each of which could go a long way toward making camping a more enjoyable experience. Inexperienced campers may also misjudge the weather and forget to pack things, such as extra blankets, sleeping bags, and heaters.

Which of the following sentences contains the main idea of this passage?

(A) First-time campers may forget things, such as insect repellent, extra matches, and toilet tissue, each of which could go a long way toward making camping a more enjoyable experience.

(B) Most areas of virgin, untapped, and undeveloped wilderness are natural habitats for several creatures.

(C) When critters cross paths with campers, especially inexperienced campers, mayhem is bound to occur.

(D) Camping in the wilderness can be a harrowing experience for people who are unfamiliar with the outdoors.

2. Every day, thousands of crimes are attempted in every state in America. Unfortunately, some of them are successful. Thankfully, though, many crimes are foiled, not by the police but by the wanna-be criminals themselves. Some real-life examples of such crimes are listed here. The names of the perpetrators have been withheld so the morons are not embarrassed any more than they have been embarrassed already.

Once there was a thief who broke into a store through the roof, fell to the floor, and broke his leg; he had to call 911 to get help.

Another thief broke into the home of a vacationing family and entered the home through the garage. Inside, the family's German shepherd cornered the intruder for three days!

Here's another: A thief dropped his wallet during a burglary; the next day, he called the police to see if anyone had turned it in. What do you think happened to him?

Every day, hundreds of would-be hot-check writers steal someone else's checks, then sign their own names to the stolen checks to cash them!

Many criminals foil their own plans because they make dumb decisions.

Which of the following sentences contains the main idea of the paragraph?

(A) Every day, thousands of crimes are attempted in every state in America.

(B) Thankfully, though, many crimes are foiled, not by the police but by the wanna-be criminals themselves.

(C) Many criminals foil their own plans because they make dumb decisions.

(D) Some real-life examples of such crimes are listed here.

How Wise?

1. (D) Camping in the wilderness can be a harrowing experience for people who are unfamiliar with the outdoors.

2. (C) Many criminals foil their own plans because they make dumb decisions.

chapter 9

Hey, Where's the Big Idea, Again?

Sometimes the author doesn't include the main idea of a reading passage in the text. Perhaps the author is trying to be clever, is trying to be artistic, and perhaps, occasionally, was absent-minded and forgot to include it in the text.

Hey, what's the big idea? Or should I say where's the big idea? Didn't we already do this?

No, Chi, not at all. Remember the hints we gave you earlier about trying to imagine or picture the passage in your mind? Remember that we said to try to imagine the outcome of the passage even before you get to the end? These tricks are really all you need. If you are reading a passage and you don't see a sentence that just spells it out for you, ask yourself two things:

> "What is the author trying to say here?"
>
> *and*
>
> "What would be one sentence that could sum up the whole passage?"

Remember that the whole point of the paragraph is to support the main idea.

So if there's no main idea, all you have are a bunch of details.

That's so right, Chi! And then all you have to do is figure out what the heck those details support.

Let's look at an example.

> Saturday was cold and rainy, so the family, with nothing else better to do, decided to clean the house. The mother, the father, and even the 2-year-old were in on the action. The mother tackled the kitchen first. She washed four loads of dirty dishes in the dishwasher and cleaned three weeks' worth of expired milk, eggs, and mystery meats out of the refrigerator. She scraped who-knows-what off the stovetop and chiseled baked-on cheese out of the oven. Even the toddler knew something important was going on. Meanwhile, the father picked up the mountains of dirty clothes lying throughout the house. He pulled shoes, dirty socks, and old pizza boxes from beneath the bed. He washed

load after load of dirty laundry. The toddler began to get excited, and he picked up his building blocks, one by one, and placed them in his toy chest, while watching his parents with wonder. Finally, after about an hour of cleaning and straightening, the toddler couldn't stand it anymore. He toddled over and asked his mother, "Mommy, who's coming over today?"

That is *so* cute. So who *was* coming over? I bet it was Mrs. Smith, the nosy next-door neighbor. She can see the dust in our house from her kitchen window! I can just picture it.

That's good, Chi, that you can picture it; that's exactly what we want. Go back and skim through the passage and find the main idea. On second thought, don't waste your time, because the passage doesn't have a main idea that you can see. The main idea is *implied*. In other words, the main idea isn't written out for you—it's hinted at indirectly. Can you think of what the main idea for this passage might be? Look at this list of possibilities, and see if you can pick the sentence that best fits as the *implied* main idea of the previous passage.

(A) The family hates to clean, so they only clean the house on Saturdays.

(B) The family is expecting someone important Saturday night.

(C) The family cleans so rarely that the toddler assumes that company is coming any time his parents clean up the house.

(D) The parents need the toddler's help so that he can feel as if he's part of the family.

The best choice from the selections above is **(C)**: The family cleans so rarely that the toddler assumes that company is coming any time his parents clean up the house. Remember that the main idea is supported by the other sentences in the paragraph.

Let's do another and see if it's any easier the second time around.

My friends and I always make plans to watch the Super Bowl together every year. We grill burgers, eat potato chips, and have a great time. We get fired up and whipped into a football-induced frenzy before the game even starts. All the guys jump around, give each other high-fives, and carry on like a bunch of big kids. For us, it's the biggest day of the sporting world's calendar of events. My girlfriend invites her friends over for a Super Bowl party every year, too. They just watch the commercials.

My buddies and I all watch the game, then run to the kitchen during the commercials and sprint back to the living room so we don't miss any action. My girlfriend and her friends watch the commercials while we're in the kitchen grabbing food, and then they hang out in my bedroom painting their nails or whatever during the good stuff.

Boy, his girlfriend and her friends must be really smart. Couldn't they just watch the commercials at that department store that sells TVs in the mall? That way they could *multitask*!

Guess you're not a football fan, Chi. But maybe you can tell us what the implied main idea was in the passage from the following choices.

(A) Although for different reasons, the Super Bowl encourages strange behavior in both men and women.

(B) Although for different reasons, the Super Bowl appeals to both sports fans and non-sports fans.

(C) The Super Bowl provides great opportunities for fellowship, bonding, togetherness, and relationship building.

(D) The Super Bowl does not rock!

That's easy; it's (D)! Ok, I'm kidding. I know it's really (B). Can't fault me for trying, right?

In any case, Chi, choice **(B)** would make a great first sentence for the paragraph. It mentions that the Super Bowl appeals to two types of people—sports fans and non-sports fans, and then the paragraph supports that idea.

Let's review and then do a review exercise. Remember these things before you begin:

- ★ An implied main idea is just like the main idea of any other passage; it is supported by all the other sentences' details.
- ★ To identify an implied main idea, ask yourself, "What is the author trying to say here?" and "What would be one sentence that could sum up the whole passage?"

Get Wise!

1. Some people bite their fingernails. Biting your fingernails in the privacy of your home is bad enough, but biting your fingernails in public places is extremely irritating. I can't listen to that constant *click, click, click* of those fingernails hitting the floor. Another bad habit I can't stand is knuckle cracking. I get totally creeped out when I hear someone cracking his or her knuckles. Usually, it's some big guy, and I'm not brave enough to tell him to stop. Yet another bad habit I can't stand is when people chew with their mouths open. Nobody wants to see what their food looks like after it's been mashed by their molars. Worst of all, for me, is blowing the nose. Nearly everyone is grossed out by that behavior. Why do people do things like that?

Which of the following contains the main idea of the previous passage?

(A) Everybody has bad habits.

(B) Some people have bad habits that are not only disgusting but also annoying to others.

(C) Some people try to gross people out every chance they get.

(D) A bad habit is hard to break.

2. If you are in a hurry to get ready in the morning, chances are that you won't be able to find your belt or the left shoe from the pair you want to wear. It's as if some cosmic force were working against you. Once you get dressed, your dog will probably choose that opportunity to get out of the yard and run down the street and into your neighbor's backyard. If you have to chase the dog, you have to count on getting hot and sweaty and getting your pants dirty. Now that you are really in a hurry, you probably won't be able to find your car keys. If you find your car keys, you'll probably have difficulty starting your car. Once you get your car moving, you can count on one-lane traffic because of construction. Additionally, you can probably expect to be driving behind an 80-year-old woman who has been driving the same speed since 1940. The same person probably has her left turn signal on the entire time, too. If you make it through the construction, you'll have to stop at every red light along the way. If you make it through the traffic lights, count on the police officer waiting in her car on the side of the road, setting up a speed trap.

So here's an idea: If you're in a hurry, take the time to think of all the things that will go wrong and just take your time, instead.

Which of the following is the main idea of the passage?

(A) Cosmic forces are aligned against you.

(B) When you are in a hurry, things have a way of going wrong and slowing you down.

(C) Things can go badly on Friday the thirteenth.

(D) Traffic can be hectic, especially if you are short on time.

How Wise?

1. **(B)** Some people have bad habits that are not only disgusting but also annoying to others.

2. **(B)** When you are in a hurry, things have a way of going wrong and slowing you down.

chapter 10

A Textbook Example

Finding the main idea in a textbook may be the easiest of all the types of reading passages you'll encounter, because textbooks are generally organized using an outline format. For example, textbooks are broken into chapters, with each chapter being an entire collection of information about a particular subject or theme. Within each chapter, the information is broken down into smaller groupings of information. Generally speaking, in each chapter of a textbook, the main idea is presented first, followed by all the supporting information and details. That should make it pretty darn simple to find the main idea in a textbook. Just remember, though, that a textbook is so full of information that when you are reading a textbook for real you can't just zip through it. You'll need to slow down so that you catch all the details. Remember that your reading speed should be slow when reading a textbook.

You know, I think I may have a textbook or two somewhere in the bottom of my locker.

Let's take a look at an example from a textbook. How about an excerpt from everyone's favorite subject? Math!

> A *set* is a group of related things, objects, letters, or numbers known as *members* or *elements*. It is usually named by an uppercase italic letter, such as Set *F*, but may be named just by its description. For example, 3 is a member of the set of odd counting numbers; 3 is also an element of real numbers. It follows, then, that the set of odd counting numbers must be a *subset* of the set of real numbers, because the latter must contain even numbers as well as odd ones.

Yikes! I think I need that *Get Wise! Mastering Math Skills* book.

The good news, Chi, is that we won't ask you if you understand the math stuff. Remember how we said that textbooks are organized? Then it stands to reason that the **first** sentence will contain the main idea. Even if you don't fully grasp the content, the rest of the paragraph clearly provides additional information about the first sentence. Let's look at a paragraph from another subject, and we'll see if it works the same way. Remember to read it slowly and concentrate not only on the main idea but also on the facts and details in the paragraph.

Do you have anything about fashion or entertainment? Those I totally understand.

According to Italian chemist Amedeo Avogadro, the number **6.02×10^3** is the number of formula units in a pure sample of substance with a mass that is numerically equal to the formula weight in grams. OK, so in layman's terms, **Avogadro's number** allows chemists to signify particles too small to be seen and counted directly. Therefore, Avogadro's number could represent 6.2×10^{23} of material, like the sugar particles of a powdered sugar doughnut or, in the field of chemistry, atoms. So 1 g of carbon atoms contains the same number of atoms as 44 g of carbon dioxide atoms. The mass of material in grams is equal to the atomic or formula weight and can now be expressed as a **mole** of that material. The number of atoms or molecules in a mole of material is Avogadro's number. A mole unit of any substance is a sample of proportions that can be seen, used, and manipulated in a laboratory. So the mole (abbreviated mol) is the formula weight in grams.

I thought an Avogadro was what you used to make guacamole!

Regardless of whether you grasp everything that is mentioned in this passage, you can see again that the first sentence contains the main idea and the rest of the sentences contain facts and details that support and explain the main idea. Unfortunately for Chi, the paragraph did not contain a recipe for guacamole or a celebrity sighting. It did, however, contain several facts and information that would need to be circled, highlighted, or underlined if you were studying the passage. Let's look at one more example from a textbook, an excerpt on Canadian history.

Well, I like Shania Twain, and I *love* Canadian bacon on my pizza.

In the late eighteenth and early nineteenth centuries, two companies battled for control of the fur trade and sparked westward expansion in Canada. The Hudson Bay Company had been granted a monopoly on the fur trade, but a company founded by French-Canadian fur traders defied the monopoly. The North West Company explored, mapped, and tapped the natural resources of Canada all the way to the Pacific Coast. Both companies struggled for influence throughout the western territories. Friction between the two companies often resulted in outbreaks of violence in frontier towns. Finally, in 1821, the two companies merged and the Hudson Bay Company assumed control of the Canadian fur trade. However, by the end of the nineteenth century, the timber industry replaced the fur trade as the leading industry in Canada.

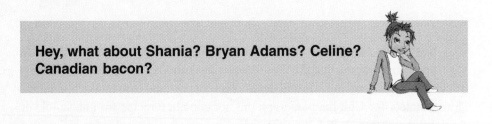

Hey, what about Shania? Bryan Adams? Celine? Canadian bacon?

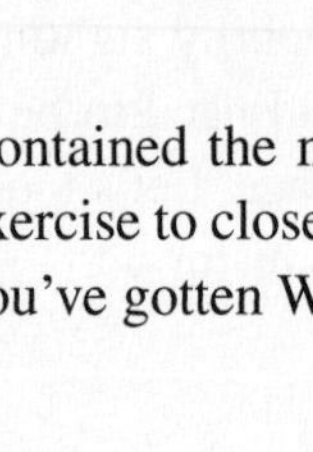

Not now, Chi, maybe later. Again, the first sentence contained the main idea. You definitely have the hang of this. Let's do a review exercise to close the book, so to speak, on this chapter, but not before we see if you've gotten Wise!

Get Wise!

1. Just as we are pulled by gravity, so, too, are landmasses. Gravity pulls on rocks and soil, sending them down slopes in an action called **mass wasting**. Rapid mass wasting occurs in the form of landslides and mudslides. **Landslides** result when earthquakes loosen soil or when rainwater pushes rocks down a slope. **Mudslides** occur after heavy rains or when volcanic eruptions cause snow to melt off the top of mountains.

Which of the following sentences best states the main idea of the previous passage?

(A) Gravity causes landslides and mudslides.

(B) The force of gravity is a constant on Earth—and it plays a role in erosion.

(C) Erosion is a major cause of the loss of landmass on Earth.

(D) Landmasses cause gravitational pull and, therefore, cause erosion on Earth.

2. Supply can be defined as all the goods available regardless of price. Demand can be defined as consumers' desires to purchase goods. Producers must place prices on the goods that are high enough so that they will make a profit after paying for all the production costs. Consumers seek to pay the lowest price possible for goods. Producers must set the amount of production based on the demand for goods. The price and the availability of goods determine the demand. These factors working together make up the principle of supply and demand.

Which of the following sentences best states the main idea of the previous passage?

(A) The primary force, and one of the basic principles of economics, is that of supply and demand.

(B) Consumers can be fickle, and their fickleness determines both supply and demand in the complicated world of economics.

(C) Supplying the demand for consumers helps produce goods at a fixed price, particularly in a mixed economy.

(D) Demanding a supply for consumers helps production calculate the economic benefits of mass-market advertising.

How Wise?

1. **(B)** The force of gravity is a constant on Earth—and it plays a role in erosion.

2. **(A)** The primary force, and one of the basic principles of economics, is that of supply and demand.

Extra! Extra! Read All About It!

How often do you read the newspaper? If you read the newspaper regularly, you're already ahead of the game. It doesn't matter whether you read the international, national, state, or local news. It doesn't matter if you read fashion, sports, or the financial news. However, reading the personal ads, comics, or horoscopes probably won't help you here. Newspaper articles are written in a little different manner from other things you might read.

First of all, the subject of the article is given in the title. Second, the main idea of the article isn't necessarily in the first sentence of the article. Remember that crazy article about the world's oldest twins? Third, newspaper articles are usually written in small sections, and even the paragraphs are short. All these differences don't necessarily make it more difficult to find the main idea, though. You already know how to pick out the most important information. You already have a darn good idea about how to identify the main idea, either written or implied. Remember that you can probably read an article at medium to quick speed.

Gee, I was hoping my experience reading the comics would help me here. Bummer!

Abuse in the Office

City Councilwoman Fran Filben declined comment in response to the accusations of an office-supply abuse scandal that has rocked City Hall in recent weeks. According to sources inside City Hall, Councilwoman Filben has been advised by her attorney to remain silent during the course of the investigation.

Three weeks ago, county landfill managers reported finding staplers, desks, pencil sharpeners, telephones, and other office equipment, all showing signs of abuse and bearing the registration numbers of City Hall, strewn across the landfill.

An independent investigation has uncovered some evidence that an entire building full of type A personalities, coupled with an unusual amount of coffee consumption in the building, may be leading to mistreatment of office supplies at City Hall. Monty Moosehead, spokesperson for the independent counsel that is conducting the investigation, commented, "The scars on the staplers and the phones are simply the worst I've seen in my career. And I've been doing this kind of work for years. It's unsettling."

Protestors outside City Hall carried picket signs that read, "Stop the violence" and "They're defenseless—leave them alone!"

City Hall is facing a public relations nightmare, the office-supply abuse scandal, which is the biggest to hit City Hall since the "Keep-off-grass" scandal in the early 1980s.

That is so unfair. Is there a group I can join to help fight for the rights of office supplies?

Try to focus, Chi. As you read through the article, you should have noticed a few main things. First of all, the paragraphs were short and sweet. In fact, they are much shorter than the paragraphs you have to write for English class. Second, the main idea was *not* located in the first sentence of the article. Speaking of the main idea, did you *find* the main idea? The main idea is the last sentence of the entire article. In newspaper articles, that's not unusual. Let's do an article of a different nature, just to help you to get a feel for newspaper articles of different types.

New Season's News

Oranges, pinks, mauves, salmons, violets, magentas, and more. Get used to seeing these shades on lips this season. Fashion editor Yuluk Fabbilis says that the latest trend in lip color is the use of colors with a pink or orange tint. The more salmon, the better, he says.

"Expect to see some marvelous faces this season. The runways in Paris and New York and Milan are full of fresh new faces, and they are all wearing these new shades," said Fabbilis.

Market critics have cried foul, claiming that there is a conspiracy in the works that is fueling the new interest in these wild and crazy colors. "Fabbilis is full of bologna," remarked a cynical critic who wished to remain anonymous.

Fabbilis denied any involvement in a conspiracy and had these remarks for the critics, "Blah, blah, blah."

Now we're getting somewhere! Just the other day, I was trying to get Farah to try that new lipstick color I saw in a magazine. The article said it was that new "flounder" shade Fabbilis was talking about. Wait a minute, maybe it was "salmon." It was some kind of fishy color. She wasn't having it, though. Whatever.

Back to the article, Chi. This one was organized differently. The main idea was neither in the first sentence nor at the end of the article. The sentence with the main idea is "Fashion editor Yuluk Fabbilis says that the latest trend in lip color is the use of colors with a pink or orange tint." Every other sentence of the article, including the first sentence, gives details that support the main idea. Generally speaking, that's how newspaper articles work. Don't forget that you should be able to read through such articles quickly.

If you are reading an article from a periodical, such as a magazine or scholarly journal, the text will probably be organized in such a manner that the main idea will be toward the beginning. A magazine, such as a news magazine or fashion magazine, requires nothing more than medium to quick reading. On the other hand, a scholarly journal will be organized much like a textbook and will require a slow read.

Let's take a look at a few examples of newspaper articles in our chapter review. Read the articles, and make sure you are looking for the main idea in each.

If I nail these, you can call me the "Genuine Article!" I'm so funny.

Get Wise!

1. The Muenster County Charity Society (MCCS) is excited, really excited. Its members are jumping for joy about the headliner who will be performing in January at the Charity Ball. The MCCS has announced that its annual Charity Ball will be held this year on January 20 and also has announced that Jerry Lee Lewis will be headlining this year's musical show. The announcement came at the MCCS press conference yesterday at the American Legion Hall. The Charity Ball, as always, is being held at the Muenster County American Legion Hall.

Lou Ann Angus, spokeswoman for MCCS, said that the theme for this year's ball will be "Sock Hopping at the Hall." "We're real happy about Jerry Lee helping us rock 'n roll the night away this year. We're just real happy, and we hope you can come out and support our cause."

Angus said that the tickets for the Charity Ball will be $50 in advance and $55 at the door. For ticket information, call 1-800-555-RNRL.

Which of the following sentences contains the main idea of the article?

(A) Lou Ann Angus, spokeswoman for MCCS, said that the theme for this year's ball will be "Sock Hopping at the Hall."

(B) The Muenster County Charity Society is excited, really excited.

(C) The MCCS has announced that its annual Charity Ball will be held this year on January 20 and also has announced that Jerry Lee Lewis will be headlining this year's musical show.

(D) The Charity Ball, as always, is being held at the Muenster County American Legion Hall.

2. After a tough loss in the state semifinals, the coach had a little time to reflect on the season. "It is a tough loss to handle, but we can be proud of the great year we've had."

The Lady Vikings, despite their semifinal loss, put together a terrific 27–8 season. The Lady Vikings, after making a run at the state championship last year that fell short in the semis, worked all year to get back to the state tournament. "That was our main goal all season long," said Coach Lewis.

As a warm-up for district play, the Lady Vikings endured a rigorous schedule, which included top-notch competition and four tournaments. The small school team repeatedly knocked off bigger schools and won two tournaments in the process. Once in district play, the Lady Vikings ran the table and finished undefeated in district competition.

The Lady Vikings were the only Final Four team from a year ago to return to the Big Dance.

Which of the following sentences contains the main idea of the article?

(A) The Lady Vikings were the only Final Four team from a year ago to return to the Big Dance.

(B) "That was our main goal all season long," said Coach Lewis.

(C) After a tough loss in the state semifinals, the coach had a little time to reflect on the season.

(D) The Lady Vikings, despite their semifinal loss, put together a terrific 27–8 season.

How Wise?

1. **(C)** The MCCS has announced that its annual Charity Ball will be held this year on January 20 and also has announced that Jerry Lee Lewis will be headlining this year's musical show.

2. **(D)** The Lady Vikings, despite their semifinal loss, put together a terrific 27–8 season.

chapter 12

Name That Tune, Sort of

A long time ago, way back before you were born, maybe even when your parents were your age or younger, there was a crazy game show on television called *Name That Tune*. The idea was for the contestants to listen to a little piece of music and then try to name the song. It was all the rage for a while way back in the day.

And that has *what* to do with reading comprehension?

OK, totally legit question. Just bear with us. The funny thing about some songs is that sometimes the title of the song either is never mentioned in the song or has little or nothing to do with the song.

Now, where exactly is this going?

Here's where we're going with this. Granted, it's kind of a stretch, but we're going to do some more practice with comprehension, specifically with identifying the main idea. In this chapter, we're going to look at some passages that don't have the main idea in them. Instead of finding a sentence that contains the main idea, you're going to do something a little different. We're going to give you some passages that might be typical of a work of fiction or maybe even narrative nonfiction. You will then have to choose the best title for the passage. Instead of naming that tune, you are going to name that reading passage. Remember that we're still working on reading comprehension, and this is great practice. This kind of exercise is a common thing on standardized tests, so it will be good practice for you. Besides, we'll make it fun for you.

Let's do one for practice. Read the following passage. It won't have a main idea included in a thesis sentence or topic sentence. As you read it, try to imagine the scene as it unfolds. After you complete the passage, try to see the "big picture." You should still try to figure out the main idea. Just remember that you will be picking the best title for the passage, not the best sentence with the main idea. Here's how it will look:

> My friends invited me over for a night of cards, pizza, and female bonding. I had nothing better to do, so I said "OK." When I arrived at my friend's house, everyone was already waiting for me. They invited me over to the table and said, "Let's play Shuckle, a new card game." I agreed, and we started playing. The dealer dealt three cards to each player. Everyone looked at her cards. If any player had cards that, when put next to one another, matched her IQ, that player yelled "Shuckle" and won the game. Nobody had a match, so we kept going. The dealer dealt each player one more card. If any player could match her cards to the day and month of her birth, that player yelled

"Shuckle" and won the game. Nobody had a match, so we kept going. The dealer dealt each player one more card. This time we were trying to match the cards with our ZIP Code. Again, nobody had a match, so we kept going. The dealer dealt each player one more card. This time we were trying to match the cards with the day, month, and last two digits of the year we were born. You guessed it—no matches, so we kept going. The dealer dealt everyone two more cards, and we tried to match our phone numbers. This continued, and we tried our social security numbers and our telephone numbers with area codes. When no one won, the dealer said, "Everybody want to play again?" I politely declined and ran as fast as I could out the door. No more Shuckle for me.

Which of the following is the best title for the previous passage?

(A) "A Great Night of Bonding with the Girls"

(B) "The World's Most Boring Card Game"

(C) "Winner Takes All"

(D) "Chips, Pizza, and Loads of Fun"

No Shuckle for me, either. Where do people come up with this stuff?

Do you have a pretty good idea of how everything went down in the story? Can you picture the scene? Call us crazy, but the story could hardly be called "A Great Night of Bonding with the Girls," so it can't be choice **(A)**. Nobody won the game, so it can't be **(C)**, and there wasn't much fun, so it can't be choice **(D)**. Besides, have you ever heard of a more boring game than shuckle? We haven't. It must be choice **(B)**, "The World's Most Boring Card Game."

Let's skip all the small talk and do another exercise. Remember to try to picture the scene in your mind. Try to think of what the main idea might be as you read. Read at a medium to quick speed, and you'll be in great shape.

Get Wise!

Parents of teenagers today often roll their eyes and shake their heads at the "crazy" music that is popular today. However, they, too, were scoffed at by their parents for the "sinful rock and roll" that they listened to when they were young. Apparently, your parent's parents forgot that the big-band music and dance clubs were shocking in their day. Heck, even your great-grandparents were considered rebellious for their participation in the wild and crazy "flapper" craze. Every generation has faced such friction. Can't you just imagine hundreds of years ago parents scoffing at their kids for swooning over musicians such as Mozart and Liszt? Granted, today's rock stars and pop stars wear clothing different from the stars of the 1950s and 1960s, but society, in general, considered Elvis Presley's hip shaking absolutely horrifying.

Which of the following is the best title for the previous passage?

(A) "Rock and Roll Will Never Die"

(B) "Parents Hate Their Kids' Music and Always Have"

(C) "The Music Is Too Loud"

(D) "I Wanna Rock"

How Wise?

(B) "Parents Hate Their Kids' Music and Always Have"

chapter 13

Reading Between the Lines

Imagine, if you will, a teacher standing before a literature class instructing that class to read a particular piece of literature. The teacher goes on to tell the class that the author has implied something in the text that just isn't out there in plain view. To find the implied or possibly hidden meaning, explains the teacher, read between the lines. By the end of the class, everybody in the class has finished the assignment—everybody, that is, except for the linebacker sitting in the back row. Now imagine that linebacker straining his eyes and holding the page up to the light trying desperately to find some hidden message or code literally between the printed lines of the passage. Can't you just picture that?

Hey, that sounds like my ex-boyfriend, Matt. How do you know him?

We don't, Chi. To avoid any other confusion, let's be clear about exactly what it means to "read between the lines." To read between the lines, you'll need to practice with a passage and see what the author is saying. Then, you'll need to figure out what the author is *really* saying. Let's pretend for a moment that you received the following letter from your significant other:

> Hi. It's me. I know this is going to be tough for you, but I think maybe we should see other people or something. It's not you—it's me. You're great, but I just think we need a little space. Besides, you're too good for me, and you deserve somebody better.

Wait a minute! You *do* know Matt! Wait 'til I see him.

We promise, it's not from Matt. It's from somebody else. Anyway, what the author of the letter is trying to say is, "I found somebody else," "I don't want to be around you anymore," and "I can't think of a better way to say it, so I'm just going to tell you I'm not good enough for you so maybe you'll let me off easy." By the way, we deal with those kinds of issues in *Get Wise! Mastering Relationship Skills,* which is slated for release next Valentine's Day (just kidding).

When you're trying to read between the lines, you're trying to find the *main idea* of the passage, and then you're trying to find the main idea that is *implied*. The trick is that the implied main idea in such a passage has a little twist of some sort. Maybe it's sarcasm. Maybe it's cynicism. Maybe it's humor. Your job is to figure out what is hidden in the text. Let's look at another example:

> I read the book, and I really didn't have the feeling that I connected with the author. The author seemed vague and ambiguous. Everybody else raved about the book, but I just didn't find it to be too stimulating. The author tried to use lots of big words and fancy phrases, but the author just didn't pull it off. It wasn't convincing at all. I can't recommend this book to anyone.

So what do you think the author is really saying here? Did the author of this passage really dislike the book? Was the author of the passage so much more intelligent than the author of the book that he or she was really bored with the book? Or did the author of this passage just not get it? Perhaps by reading between the lines you will see that the author is simply saying, "I have no idea what everyone else saw in that book, because I have no idea what the book is talking about." That's what this passage is saying between the lines.

You've practiced quite a bit with finding the main idea, both implied and in plain view. Remember that you probably are not going to try to read between the lines in a textbook. A textbook is going to be cut and dry and straightforward; also, the author of a textbook wants to be sure that you have the important information.

So where might you encounter a passage in which you will need to read between the lines? Many passages of literature will require you to read between the lines if you really want to know what the author is saying. Memos may be ambiguous and not spell out things for you, so you'll need to read between the lines. With some newspaper articles, especially editorials and opinion columns, you will need to read between the lines.

Let's look at another passage so you can get a better grasp of this concept. Read the following memo, and then answer the question that follows.

MEMORANDUM

For: All employees of Kingsbury Office Building

Date: Today **Subject:** Dress Code

The management of the businesses in the Kingsbury Building has, in the past, been rather lenient regarding the office dress code. The managers and supervisors have always been flexible regarding the dress code as outlined in the building's employee handbook. Management has been especially lenient regarding the Casual Friday dress code. Management hopes that it can continue to be flexible with enforcement of the dress code and that all employees will continue to cooperate.

Which of the following is the best interpretation of the previous passage?

(A) Management does not like Casual Fridays.

(B) If employees want to enjoy continued flexible and lenient enforcement of the dress code, they should be responsible and not abuse the flexibility of the code.

(C) The dress code should be enforced much more strictly.

(D) The building is a nicer place because of the dress code.

Stop beating around the bush. All they had to say was, "Don't embarrass yourselves. Look in the mirror before you leave for work!"

You got it, Chi. That's exactly what we're talking about. Just try to find the implied main idea, and you're on the right track. Sometimes the main idea is written between the lines, because, as Chi pointed out, the author doesn't want to come right out and say something. Sometimes the author is being artistic and mysterious. Regardless of an author's intent, your ability to read between the lines and figure out what an author is saying is a great skill to have in a class, on an examination, or on a Sunday morning reading the newspaper. Let's get a little more practice reading between the lines before we move on to the next chapter.

Get Wise!

1. To all employees of Vanguard Manufacturing:

   Management has gone to great lengths to provide ample parking for all employees, support and maintenance personnel, and management. The parking spaces near the entrance of the building have been reserved for management, the spaces near the plant have been reserved for maintenance and support personnel, and the spaces behind the building and across the street have been reserved for all other employees. The parking spaces have all been marked accordingly. In addition, the spaces have been numbered and all employees have been assigned a numbered space. If this system is going to work, **all** employees must abide by the parameters of the system. Employees are encouraged to observe not only parking zones but also the numbering system. Management does not wish to make this a bigger issue than it has to be but is committed to maintaining order in the system. Employees are respectfully urged to park only in assigned spaces.

Which of the following is the best interpretation of the previous passage?

(A) Employees who are parking in other employees' parking spaces are facing fines and perhaps even termination.

(B) Some Vanguard employees have been abusing the parking system; the system will work only if employees cooperate or if management steps in and tightens control of the system.

(C) The Vanguard parking system is unfair to all employees other than management.

(D) Vanguard parking spaces should be assigned either alphabetically or according to tenure and seniority.

2. Dear Applicant,

Thank you for your résumé, your application, and your interest in employment with our company. First, let me congratulate you for getting everything cleared up with both your previous employer and the sheriff's department. The employment committee has reviewed your information and has deliberated at length. As always, the hiring process is a long and complicated one. We have had more applicants for the position you're seeking than for any other position we've ever had available. At this time, the hiring committee has decided that perhaps you may be more qualified for other positions in our company. The hiring committee encourages you to reapply for any number of positions. Thank you for your interest, and we wish you the best of luck.

Sincerely,

U. R. Aluser, Director of Personnel

Which of the following is the best interpretation of the previous passage?

(A) You aren't qualified for this job, so you aren't getting this job.

(B) You are overqualified, and we simply can't afford to hire such a quality person for this position.

(C) We have no positions open for you at this time. Apply again in a few years.

(D) We wouldn't hire you if you were the last candidate on earth.

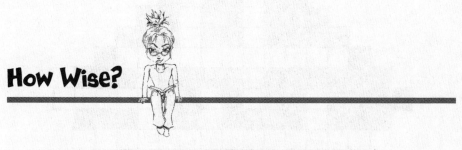

How Wise?

1. **(B)** Some Vanguard employees have been abusing the parking system; the system will work only if employees cooperate or if management steps in and tightens control of the system.

2. **(A)** You aren't qualified for this job, so you aren't getting this job.

Puzzle 2

Complete the following puzzle using the words you just learned in Chapters 6–13. Puzzle solutions are in the back of the book.

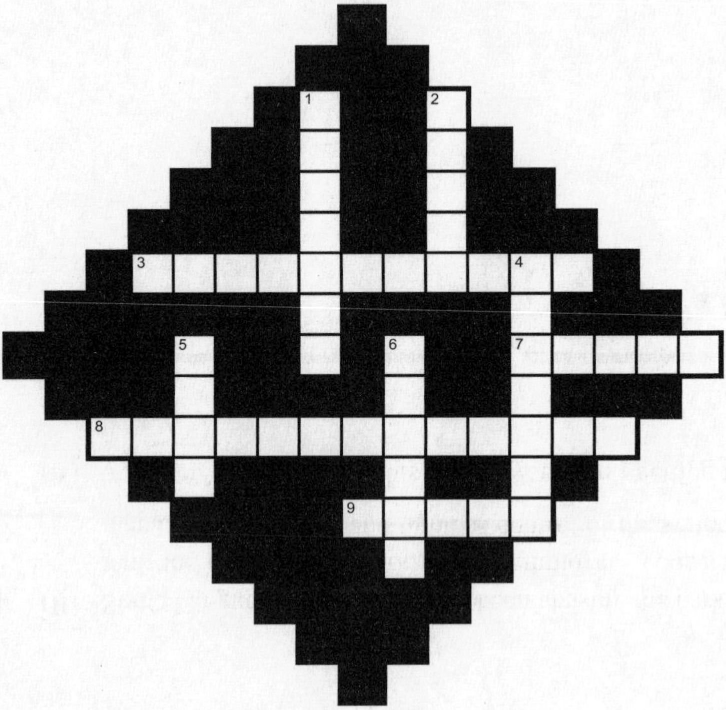

Across

3. USING YOUR BRAIN TO TRY TO VISUALIZE A READING PASSAGE

7. NAME FOR SENTENCE THAT CONTAINS THE MAIN IDEA

8. UNDERSTANDING DEEPER THAN JUST RECALL

9. PART OF A NEWSPAPER ARTICLE THAT USUALLY CONTAINS THE MAIN IDEA

Down

1. WHEN AN AUTHOR HINTS AT THE MAIN IDEA INSTEAD OF WRITING IT OUT
2. THE SENTENCE THAT IS USUALLY THE TOPIC SENTENCE IN A TEXTBOOK PARAGRAPH
4. FORMAT IN WHICH MOST TEXTBOOKS ARE ORGANIZED
5. A LETTER FROM YOUR BOSS
6. STATEMENT THAT IS THE MAIN IDEA

Chapter 14

Putting It All Together

Every now and then, especially when you're learning some new skills, it's important to stop, catch your breath, and refresh your memory a little. Up to this point, we've focused on skills you're going to need for recall and comprehension.

Gee, that's funny. I don't recall any of that.

Very funny, Chi. Seriously, though, we've looked at recall skills and comprehension skills. Hopefully they worked better for you than they did for Chi. Let's go back and quickly review what we learned about identifying important information. After all, you can't very well recall information if you don't identify it first. Here are some pointers for identifying important information in a reading passage:

- Round up some reading tools, such as a pen or pencil, ruler, or notepad.
- Use your "writing stick" or ruler to run along under the lines as you read to help you focus on the words.
- Look for information printed in **bold**, *italics,* or <u>underlined</u> text.
- Look for important information at or near the beginning of the paragraph, section, or passage.
- Look for information that is reworded and repeated.
- Look for information that is repeated and reworded. (Ha! Gotcha again!)
- Look for information that is modified by superlatives, such as *most*, *best*, or *least.*
- Look for information that is modified by absolutes, such as *always*, *all*, *never,* or *none.*

After you identify the information, your challenge is to recall the information either immediately for a test question or later for a test or to prove to your mother that you read it. Here's another little tip for both identifying and remembering important information: as you read, ask yourself *what*, *where*, *when*, *how,* and *who*? We learned several strategies for making the information stick in your brain. Do you remember them? Check your memory against our little checklist:

- Rewrite important information, preferably in your notebook.
- Jot down notes in the margin.
- Use your "writing stick" to circle or underline information.
- Use a highlighter to highlight the important information.
- Use your "writing utensil" to draw arrows from one piece of information to other relevant bits of information.

After you have these strategies committed to memory, you have to give some consideration to what you are reading. Are you reading a Hollywood gossip magazine, a calculus text, a newspaper editorial, one of the many wonderful books in the *Get Wise!* line of books (how do these shameless plugs keep getting in here?), or maybe a letter from your boss? Depending on what you are reading, you will need to adjust both your reading speed and your attention to detail. Do you remember this?

★ When reading page-turners, such as your chemistry textbook, your economics textbook, or some other textbook, slow down your reading speed and pay attention to details.

★ When reading a memo, a novel, a newspaper or magazine article, or correspondence, read at a medium speed and don't get hung up trying to remember every single fact and detail.

★ When reading a letter or an e-mail or an action-packed work of fiction or even a sappy romance novel, read at an accelerated pace and glean the general idea of the passage.

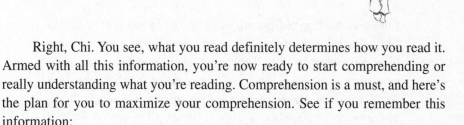

What about cereal boxes and comic books? Should I take notes?

Right, Chi. You see, what you read definitely determines how you read it. Armed with all this information, you're now ready to start comprehending or really understanding what you're reading. Comprehension is a must, and here's the plan for you to maximize your comprehension. See if you remember this information:

★ The first step toward comprehending what you read is finding the main idea.

★ The main idea of a paragraph or reading passage is often located at the beginning of the passage.

★ Occasionally, though, the main idea will be hidden in the middle or even near the end of the passage.

★ Sometimes the main idea of a passage is not even included in the passage itself; instead, it is merely implied by the author, and you will have to read the entire passage to figure out the main idea.

OK, I get the idea already!

Good! Now let's take everything we've learned so far and put it all together. So far, every time you have done a practice exercise you've only tackled one concept in each passage. In the practice exercises in this chapter, you'll be given one passage, and you'll have to use every skill you've practiced so far. You'll have to identify and recall important information. You'll have to find the main idea, regardless of whether it's spelled out for you or implied. In addition, you'll be asked to do these things while reading the passage at a particular speed. Think you can handle this? Well, what are you waiting for? Let's take a practice run. Get your reading tools together, take a deep breath, and jump right in! Read the following passage at a medium speed, and then answer the questions that follow.

> Bunko is an age-old game that is easy to learn and fun to play. Perhaps that is why it has lasted for generations. Groups gather to play Bunko but also to enjoy good company and conversation. The game dates back to the late 1800s, when it was played by groups of women, schoolchildren, and couples. It was originally known as 8-Dice Cloth. It was introduced in the United States in 1855. "Bunko Parlors" came into existence in the 1920s near the Chicago area. They were often raided by "Bunko squads" or police enforcing Prohibition. After Prohibition, Bunko playing declined, and the game moved into the suburbs. However, the game has recently resurged in popularity.

Interested in a game? Here are the rules. For starters, take twelve score sheets, and secretly draw a star on four of the sheets. Each player picks a score sheet. The four players with stars on their sheets sit at the head table. The remaining eight players sit at the middle table and the losers' table. Each table is randomly divided into two teams. Team couples sit across from each other. The game begins when the head table rings the bell. One player from each table starts the game by trying to roll ones with three dice. If one of the three dice rolls the number you are currently on, it is worth one point, two is worth two points, and three is "Bunko." If you roll three of a kind of another number, you get five points. You keep rolling until you don't roll the number that is up. Then it goes to the person to your left to take a turn. Whenever a player at the head table rolls Bunko, the bell is rung and the round stops. If the head table reaches twenty-one points before rolling Bunko, the round likewise stops. At that point, the number currently up changes to the next number (1 to 2, 2 to 3, and so on). The winning team at the head table stays there, and the losing team moves to the middle table. Everyone switches partners. The winning team at the middle table moves to the head table, and the losing team moves to the losing table. The losing team from the losing table remains there, and the winning team moves to the middle table. The new round begins with the head table ringing the bell. The game ends when four sets of Bunko are completed. When the game is over, add up your points, wins, and losses, and hand out the prizes!

Sounds about as exciting as that Shuckle game!

1. Which of the following sentences contains the main idea of the previous passage?
   - (A) After prohibition, Bunko playing declined and the game moved into the suburbs.
   - (B) When the game is over, add up your points, wins, and losses, and hand out the prizes!
   - (C) Bunko is an age-old game that is easy to learn and fun to play.
   - (D) For starters, take twelve score sheets and secretly draw a star on four of them.
2. Bunko parlors first became popular in which of the following times and places?
   - (A) New York in the 1920s
   - (B) Chicago in the 1920s
   - (C) Chicago in 1855
   - (D) The suburbs in 1855
3. How many tables does Bunko require to seat all 12 players?
   - (A) 3
   - (B) 4
   - (C) 8
   - (D) 12

Did you see the main idea in the first sentence of the passage? Go back and read it. The answer to the first question is **(C)**, because it tells you exactly what the passage is going to say. The rest of the passage supports the main idea by giving information about the age and the rules of Bunko. Now for the second question. Did you underline, circle, or highlight the dates? When you see dates, it might be a good idea to make note of them. The correct answer to the second question, if you remember from the passage, is **(B)**; the facts are there in plain view. The third and final question required a little more thought and comprehension. The passage never said: "Bunko requires ___ tables." However, it mentioned a head table, a middle table, and a losers' table. Did you catch that? That would make the correct answer **(A)**, because there are 3 tables. How'd you do? Hopefully, you were 3 for 3 on this one. Now that you get the idea, let's do a review exercise. After the review exercise, we'll move on to some more comprehension skills so that we can help you hone your reading comprehension skills even further.

Get Wise!

Read the following passages and then answer the questions that follow. Read the first passage at a slow speed and the second passage at a medium to quick speed.

> Bacteria function as **decomposers**, **nitrogen fixers**, and **symbionts**, and a small percentage are **pathogenic**. Some microbes, such as **saprophytes**, recycle dead materials and sewage into smaller molecules that can be returned to the environment. The pharmaceutical industry uses bacteria in the manufacture of antibiotics and vitamins. Many of the foods we eat, such as yogurt and cheese, are the products of bacterial metabolism. Alcohol, acids, and many other chemicals are products of bacterial cultures. Plants also benefit from relationships with bacteria. The roots of bean plants form a symbiotic relationship with bacteria that are cable of converting atmospheric nitrogen into a usable form, which not only benefits the plant but also the soil surrounding the plants. The process is known as **nitrogen fixation**. The cycling of nitrogen is achieved exclusively by bacteria.

1. Which of the following sentences is the main idea of the passage?
   (A) Many of the foods we eat, such as yogurt and cheese, are the products of bacterial metabolism.
   (B) Bacteria function as **decomposers**, **nitrogen fixers**, and **symbionts**, and a small percentage are **pathogenic**.
   (C) The implied main idea is: "Many bacteria actually serve beneficial and necessary functions to humans and to the environment."
   (D) The implied main idea is: "Bacteria can cause diseases and can be deadly to humans, plants, and animals."

2. Which of the following is *not* a product of bacteria as described in the passage?
   (A) Cheese
   (B) Carbonated beverages
   (C) Yogurt
   (D) Alcohol

3. Which of the following would be the best title for the passage?
   (A) "Bacteria: The Secret World of Helpful Creepy, Crawly Organisms"
   (B) "The Unexpected Benefits of Bacteria"
   (C) "Bacteria: A Brief History"
   (D) "Bacteria in Food"

Dear fellow PTA members,

Attached you will find a list of volunteer opportunities in the community. Many of these projects would be ideal to introduce your child to the work of volunteerism and what fulfillment giving of their time can provide. According to the Society for Growing Well-Rounded Children, volunteering with your children is the best way to develop self-confidence and a sense of leadership in your child; additionally, volunteering may help to keep your child out of trouble, and the PTA wants to emphasize this during the upcoming year. By encouraging your child to volunteer his or her time, you show that he or she is important to the community. Of a thousand 17-year-olds surveyed, only 8 had ever been encouraged to give their time for others voluntarily. We encourage you to consider how valuable a lesson your child could learn when spending an afternoon with you at a homeless shelter, a local soup kitchen, or a day care. If you have any questions, please contact Candace Cotton at 555-1217. Happy Volunteering!

Sincerely,

Patty Parker, PTA President

4. Which of the following is the main idea of the previous passage?

(A) We encourage you to consider how valuable a lesson your child could learn when spending an afternoon with you at a homeless shelter, a local soup kitchen, or a day care.

(B) According to the Society for Growing Well-Rounded Children, volunteering with your children is the best way to develop self-confidence and a sense of leadership in your child; additionally, volunteering may help keep your child out of trouble, and the PTA wants to emphasize this during the upcoming year.

(C) The PTA is volunteering to help children stay out of trouble.

(D) Volunteers do not get in trouble, especially those involved in education.

5. Which of the following was *not* mentioned as a possible volunteer opportunity for parents and children?

(A) Animal shelter

(B) Day care

(C) Homeless shelter

(D) Soup kitchen

How Wise?

1. (C) The implied main idea is: "Many bacteria serve beneficial and necessary functions to humans and to the environment."

2. (B) Carbonated beverages

3. (B) "The Unexpected Benefits of Bacteria"

4. (B) According to the Society for Growing Well-Rounded Children, volunteering with your children is the best way to develop self-confidence and a sense of leadership in your child; additionally, volunteering may help keep your child out of trouble, and the PTA wants to emphasize this during the upcoming year.

5. (A) Animal shelter

chapter 15

Gaze into Your Crystal Ball

Can you predict the future? Can you predict who will win the World Series before the season starts? Can you predict the numbers in the lottery? Can you predict what questions will be on your college entrance examination? Can you predict what kind of mood your biology teacher will be in when you get to class every day? We'll have to assume that your answer to each one of these questions is "No."

I'm gazing into my crystal ball, and I predict there's a point to these questions and you'll tell us quickly what that point is.

Yes, Chi, you're right. One of the most common reading comprehension exercises on standardized tests is predicting the outcome of a reading passage. In other words, you read a passage and then try to figure out what the logical outcome of the story would be.

This exercise is designed to see whether you have a good grasp of the passage, usually a story or a description of something that happens in a particular order. Remember several chapters ago when we recommended that you try to imagine the scene as you read? That's what you have to do if you are asked to choose the best ending or the most logical outcome in a reading passage or story. Picture the story in your imagination, and then, based on the facts that are presented and the order in which the facts are presented, picture how the story will end. Let's take a look at an example so you can see what this type of exercise might look like on a test. Read the following story, and then answer the question that follows.

> Bob decided to surprise Leslie with a funny practical joke for her birthday. Leslie was constantly playing jokes on her friends, especially on Bob. All of Leslie's friends believed the jokes were funny until they fell victim themselves. One by one Leslie's friends tried to get revenge for all the years of practical joking. Her friends got together with Bob and devised a foolproof plan to exact revenge. Bob and her friends threw Leslie a surprise party. They hid at her house and waited for her to come home from work. When she got home, her friends jumped out and yelled, "Happy birthday!" Immediately they threw their arms around her and said, "Bob has a surprise for you." Bob walked over to her as her friends held her arms. In Bob's hand was a big box with a bright yellow bow on it. Bob opened the box and pulled out a huge lemon meringue pie with whipped cream on top. Leslie knew she had been had. She begged and pleaded for Bob to set the pie on the table. Bob smiled at her while her friends grinned with delight. Leslie begged one more time for mercy.

Which of the following sentences is the most probable outcome of the previous story?

(A) Bob carefully set the pie on the table and said, "Just kidding!"

(B) Bob reached for a fork and handed it to Leslie.

(C) Bob ran as fast as he could, because he was afraid that Leslie would retaliate.

(D) Bob seized the opportunity and hit Leslie in the face with the pie, leaving her dripping with meringue and whipped cream.

Hey! I know exactly how this ends, and it isn't pretty!

Did you picture the story in your imagination as you read? Based on the facts of the story, do you have a good idea how the story would end? Let's review the facts. Everybody wanted revenge on Leslie, including Bob, so they devised a plan to get her back. If they had the chance, would they back out? Nope! Therefore, choices **(A)**, **(B)**, and **(C)** most probably aren't right. Unfortunately for Leslie, the logical and most probable answer is **(D)**. That makes sense, doesn't it? It's the next logical step.

The secret to predicting the future, at least in the future of reading passages, is twofold:

- ★ First, you have to recognize the important information in the reading passage. We know you can do that—after all, we trained you! You can't very well follow the steps in a progression if you don't know the facts.
- ★ Second, you have to see the bigger picture and have a good working knowledge or comprehension of the story. In other words, you have to do more than just visualize the reading passage one line at a time.

What about seeing the future?

Good question. To see the future, imagine that each line of the reading passage is a piece of a puzzle. You don't know what the puzzle is going to look like when you put it all together, but you have a better idea with each piece you add. As you piece together the puzzle, or read the lines of the passage, try to picture the finished product in your head. If you had a puzzle with only one piece missing, you would be able to imagine what the missing piece looks like. It would be the same with a story that was missing the ending. If you can imagine the story in your head, you can figure out the best ending for the story. It's that simple. Let's try another reading passage. This time, use the puzzle analogy to help you find the answer to the question.

Marcus had spent the last six months of his life practicing for the one goal he set for himself: to break the world record on the hottest new video game on the market, *Mission: Annihilation*. Every day after school, Marcus ran home from school, finished his homework, and turned on the video game. All weekend every weekend Marcus played the video game. Marcus's friends invited him to the movies, to ball games, and to parties, but Marcus kept his eye on the prize. Marcus was determined not to let anything or anyone stand in his way. Marcus's mother even tried to set him up with the new girl down the street. As expected, Marcus said, "No thanks." After five months, Marcus had worked his way into the world's top 10 *Mission: Annihilation* list. After six months, Marcus was on the verge of reaching the world record score. The weekend Marcus had waited for finally arrived. Marcus sat down and started the game; he had a hunch about this one. Three hours into the game, Marcus's mother went into his room and said, "Your uncle just called and said he has two extra tickets to the Blink 182 concert. Do you want to go with him tonight?"

Which of the following sentences is the most probable outcome of the previous story?

(A) Marcus turned off the video game and said, "Blink 182! I'm there!"

(B) Marcus thought long and hard before he finally turned off the game; he said, "I can start this again tomorrow."

(C) Marcus said, "No thanks," and continued playing his game.

(D) Marcus said, "No thanks," and continued playing his game; he changed his mind a few minutes later, though, and turned off the game.

Man, I'd have dropped anything to catch a Blink concert! What was he thinking?

Well, Chi, that's exactly what you should be asking. What was Marcus thinking? If you paid close attention, you noticed that all Marcus had on his mind was the game. Was there any reason to think that Marcus would put down his game for anything at all if he didn't for his friends or for a girl? Of course not. Did you pick up on the fact that Marcus "had a hunch" about this particular game? That should have really tipped you off that he was 100% committed to the game. If you picked up on these things, then you almost certainly chose choice **(C)**.

Let's do a quick review before we do a review exercise.

- ★ First, identify the important information in the passage as you read.
- ★ Second, try to imagine the events in your head as they unfold. Remember the puzzle analogy? Try to envision where the story is going and how it will end.

If you do these things, you'll have no problem figuring out how a reading passage is most likely to end.

Get Wise!

Read the following passage and answer the question that follows.

It was Homecoming night, and the stadium was full of fans. You could feel the excitement and anticipation in the air. Benedict Arnold High School had scheduled our cross-town rival, Parkview High School, as our Homecoming opponent. As was customary, the football coach always schedules the worst possible team for Homecoming to guarantee a victory for the home team. That season was no different, except that Arnold and Parkview were both 0–9 on the season. The implications were huge—the winner would avoid a 0–10 record, and the winner would have bragging rights.

Despite the wretchedness of the two teams, the game was unbelievably exciting. The game was nip and tuck until an Arnold touchdown put us ahead 19–18. With the game seemingly in hand, my coach finally put me in the game for a final defensive stand with Parkview facing fourth down and 27 yards to go on their own 49-yard line. With only 20 seconds left on the clock, Parkview ran one final play. The quarterback dropped back and fired the pass in my direction. The receiver I was defending pulled in the ball and made the catch. I ran at him as fast as I could and hit him head on. From that point on, everything seemed to happen in slow motion. I hit him, the ball popped loose, and we both hit the ground. Everyone in the stadium was screaming, "Get the ball!" I did. I scooped up the ball, and everyone screamed, "Run! Run!" I did. As I ran toward the end zone, the players, coaches, fans, and even the cheerleaders jumped up and down and flailed their arms wildly. They were yelling something at me as I sprinted toward the end zone, but I couldn't understand them. As I approached the end zone, I dove across the goal line and scored! I scored! Then the entire stadium got deathly quiet. The coaches, players, and even those cheerleaders looked at me in disbelief. I spiked the football and pointed to the scoreboard as my heart pounded in my chest.

Which of the following sentences is the most probable outcome of the previous story?

(A) The scoreboard read Arnold 25, Parkview 18—I scored, and the crowd loved me for it.

(B) The scoreboard read Arnold 19, Parkview 20, because I ran the wrong way and scored a safety for the other team; I lost the game for Arnold High.

(C) The cheerleaders mobbed me because I had proven my athletic prowess.

(D) The coach apologized to me for not playing me earlier.

How Wise?

(B) The scoreboard read Arnold 19, Parkview 20, because I ran the wrong way and scored a safety for the other team; I lost the game for Arnold High.

chapter 16

Elementary, My Dear Chi!

OK, we know what you're thinking—"Oh no, another corny chapter full of detective references!"

You read my mind! Was that from your crystal ball?

No, Chi. No crystal ball. We just know you have great recall skills now, and we know you would remember the outstanding chapter full of detective jargon. We aren't going to do that again, but that's not to say this chapter will be totally free of detective references. Besides, if you thought this was another detective chapter based on the chapter's title, then we can draw two conclusions. First, we can conclude that you are familiar with the legendary literary sleuth Sherlock Holmes. Second, we can conclude that you already have some skills in the area of drawing conclusions. Wouldn't you know it? That's what this chapter is about—drawing conclusions.

If you haven't figured it out yet, each chapter you read builds on the skills you've already learned. The same thing applies to this chapter. In this chapter, we're going to learn how to read a story or some other reading passage and then draw a conclusion based on the information in the reading passage. It probably goes without saying that you draw conclusions every day. But, have you ever given any thought about what is involved in drawing a conclusion? What makes a conclusion different from an assumption? Well, we all know what happens when we assume something, right? If not, just ask around, and you'll find out easy enough. An assumption is really just a guess, and that's not what we're shooting for in this chapter.

Let's think for a moment about conclusions. You draw conclusions every single day. When you get to school and discover that your first period teacher is extra grumpy, you conclude that she didn't get enough sleep last night. When you get to the cafeteria on Friday and find "casserole surprise" on the menu, you conclude that the casserole contains leftovers from earlier in the week. When you hear a ridiculous answer come from the back of the room during class, you conclude that the class clown gave the answer. So, what can you conclude about conclusions? Conclusions are based on facts or at least on things that you can observe. It is important to remember that conclusions are not guesses or assumptions. Conclusions must be based on something.

In a way, drawing a conclusion after reading a passage is similar to predicting how the passage will end. In both cases, you have to identify the important facts and information. After all, conclusions are based on facts. Then, you have to envision the reading passage and follow the progression of the story, events, or facts in the reading passage. You see? These are skills you've already been working on throughout this book. Let's take a look at an example of a reading passage from which you will need to draw a conclusion.

Based on what I just read, I conclude that I can so handle this with no prob!

In recent years, hundreds of major big businesses and corporations have invested millions of dollars in research concerning the effects of physical fitness programs for office personnel and white-collar workers. The researchers put thousands of office workers on strict diets and rigorous physical fitness routines. At the end of the test period, the office workers reported that they felt better about themselves and about their jobs. The office workers reported having more energy and more motivation during the workday. In addition, researchers reported that the workers' cholesterol, blood pressure, and stress levels all showed great improvement during the test period. Researchers officially recommended to the corporations that the fitness programs be continued indefinitely because of the many benefits of the physical fitness.

Which of the following is the most likely conclusion that can be drawn based on the previous reading passage?

(A) Research for corporate physical fitness programs is expensive, but the research is worth the price.

(B) Research for corporate physical fitness programs is unfair for workers who aren't chosen to participate in the programs.

(C) Office workers who are subjected to rigorous physical fitness regimens are less likely to drink coffee and eat donuts at breaks in the workday.

(D) Corporations are likely to have greater productivity from office workers who participate in physical fitness programs.

Let's first look at the facts in this passage. Based on the reading, you know that corporations paid for research on the effects of physical fitness on office workers. You can only imagine how these workers reacted at first when their bosses took away their éclairs and soft drinks and made them get on treadmills and elliptical machines. But that's beside the point. The results of the research showed that the office workers who underwent physical training felt better and felt more motivated than they did before they started exercising. If you have a company whose workers are happy, who feel good about themselves and their jobs, and who feel more motivated during the day, what do you think is the result? In the words of the great Sherlock Holmes, "It's elementary." Your company is going to be more productive, more profitable, and, in general, better off than before the exercise began. Therefore, the correct answer to the previous question has to be **(D)**. In addition, think of all the money the company can save on donuts, coffee, and vending machines full of junk food.

It's hard to argue with that!

Let's do another practice passage before we move on to the chapter review. Just like with the previous reading passage, read through the passage carefully and pay close attention to the details.

> The Beatles burst onto the American music scene in the early 1960s. Then, in copycat efforts to cash in on Beatlemania, dozens of other rock-and-roll groups formed with three or four young guys and flooded the airwaves with similar music. During the 1970s, the bands got a little older. With the 1980s, though, the bands of handsome, young boys dominated the charts again. Bands such as New Edition and New Kids on the Block were all the rage. As before, the bands' popularity died down later in the decade and early in the next decade. Then, in some strange phenomenon, boy bands made a comeback in the mid to

late 1990s. The Backstreet Boys and 'N SYNC, among others, dominated the radio and the music video scenes during the 1990s but have since cooled off. In every case, millions of young girls swooned over the young rockers.

Which of the following is the most likely conclusion that can be drawn based on the previous reading passage?

(A) Boy bands are the greatest musicians of each generation.
(B) Every decade has its own boy bands full of young, wildly appealing guys who charm the young girls into buying their albums, CDs, and concert tickets.
(C) Every time boy bands burst onto the scene, they likewise fade away after some time.
(D) Nobody really likes boy bands.

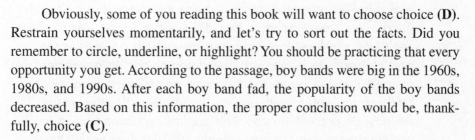

Hey, let's not hate on the boy bands! Those guys are still hot!

Obviously, some of you reading this book will want to choose choice **(D)**. Restrain yourselves momentarily, and let's try to sort out the facts. Did you remember to circle, underline, or highlight? You should be practicing that every opportunity you get. According to the passage, boy bands were big in the 1960s, 1980s, and 1990s. After each boy band fad, the popularity of the boy bands decreased. Based on this information, the proper conclusion would be, thankfully, choice **(C)**.

By now you should really have the hang of this. Again, the process of drawing conclusions is the coming together of several skills you have been sharpening throughout the course of this book. Take careful notice of the facts and details of the reading passage, because conclusions are based on that information. As the reading passage unfolds, try to see the bigger picture and try to think ahead and figure out where the passage is going. After you finish the text, look back over the information and try to find a pattern. With these steps, you can draw conclusions from most any reading passage. After all, you draw conclusions every day—just transfer those skills to reading.

Well, I don't know why you say it's elementary. My brother's in the first grade, and all he can draw are doghouses, with me inside them!

Get Wise!

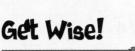

Read the following passages and answer the question that follows each.

1. We took a field trip to the zoo last week and observed several different animals that have been trained to do various things. We saw elephants that did various tricks. We saw seals and sea lions that balanced basketballs on their noses and clapped on command. The dolphins and killer whales jumped through hoops and carried divers on their backs. Without a doubt, though, the most impressive display was in the primate area of the zoo. The gorillas had been trained to use sign language to communicate with not only each other but also with their human trainers. Those gorillas knew hundreds of signs and, thus, hundreds of words. Some of the gorillas, only several years old, were younger than my little brother, and they were more capable of expression and communication than my brother.

Which of the following is the most likely conclusion that can be drawn based on the previous reading passage?

(A) The gorillas were smarter than the author's little brother.

(B) Because of their intelligence, gorillas can learn useful skills, such as sign language, rather than just learning entertaining tricks.

(C) The gorillas were the smartest animals at the zoo and were only slightly less intelligent than the humans who trained them.

(D) The gorillas could possibly teach the humans how to communicate in gorilla language if they were given enough time.

2. At the Hollywood award shows every year, the celebrities go to great lengths to dress in the latest fashions and to make fashion statements. Generally speaking, the male celebrities dress in tuxes and look pretty nice. However, the women are usually the celebrities who shock the world with sometimes elegant and sometimes awful outfits. The female celebrities have been known to wear the most hideous dresses and gowns. Each of the dresses and gowns, regardless of what everyone thinks of them, definitely makes a statement. In addition, the female celebrities often pay hundreds and even thousands of dollars to have their hair and makeup done for the award shows. Many times, though, the female celebrities' hairstyles make them look like they just woke up or like they just rode in on a motorcycle without wearing a helmet. Moreover, the makeup jobs on many of the famous women look like the makeup artists were either blind or playing a joke on the celebrities. Interestingly enough, the women never seem to mind that they look outrageous.

Which of the following is the most likely conclusion that can be drawn based on the previous reading passage?

(A) Female celebrities usually make more of an effort to make a fashion statement at award shows than do their male counterparts.

(B) Female celebrities have poor fashion sense.

(C) Male celebrities have poor fashion sense.

(D) Makeup artists and hairstylists are involved in a conspiracy to make female celebrities look bad.

How Wise?

1. **(B)** Because of their intelligence, gorillas can learn useful skills, such as sign language, rather than just learning entertaining tricks.

2. **(A)** Female celebrities usually make more of an effort to make a fashion statement at award shows than do their male counterparts.

chapter 17

Drawing Conclusions from ... Yawn ... ZZZ ...

What do comedians and textbook writers have in common? Go ahead and think about it for a minute. The answer is *nothing*! Now, before we start bashing textbook writers, it's understandable that textbooks aren't all page-turners. After all, textbooks are designed to cut to the chase and give you information, data, and cold hard facts. Textbooks aren't designed to keep you entertained, just educated. And, like it or not, you're going to have to get through an awful lot of these textbooks before you get out of high school. Then, if you want to do the college thing, too, that's more textbooks for you to read. We've talked quite a bit about finding the important information in textbooks. Now we need to put those skills to work and practice drawing conclusions from textbook passages.

I've come to the conclusion that I'll probably give up textbook reading for good as soon as I get out of college.

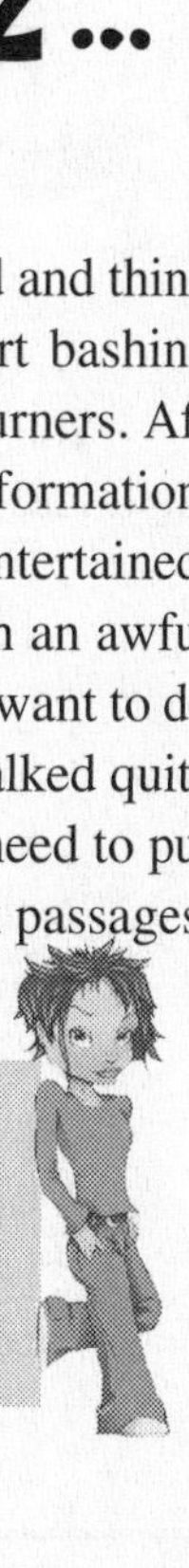

But because you have a lot more textbooks to read in your academic career, we better get started with the strategies. Remember that whenever you read a textbook, you need to slow down your reading speed so that you don't skip important information. Don't forget about your "writing utensils." You'll really need those to circle, underline, and make notes, especially with a passage from a textbook. Pay special attention to the main idea of the passage, because it may give quite a bit of insight into any conclusions that can be drawn. The main thing to remember when drawing conclusions from a textbook passage is this: textbooks are designed to be straightforward and not tricky or artistic. Therefore, drawing a conclusion from a textbook involves identifying the most important information and following the logical progression as the text proceeds. Then you simply have to put it all together and make your conclusion based on the facts. That's it.

Hey, all these strategies are pretty similar! I just have to change it up a little depending on what I'm reading and why I'm reading it. Right?

You hit the nail on the head, Chi. Because you believe you have a pretty good idea what to do, let's do a practice passage.

> The writers of the Constitution divided the United States government into three branches. The writers of the Constitution also included in the plan of government another system of safeguards. This system is known as the system of checks and balances. Each branch of government has the ability to check the power of the other two branches, and that helps balance the power of the branches. The executive branch can check the power of the legislative branch by vetoing legislation, and it can check the power of the judicial branch by appointing judges. The legislative branch can check the power of the executive branch by overriding vetoes, and it can check the power of the judicial branch

> by impeaching judges and by rejecting judicial appointments. The judicial branch can check the power of the executive branch by declaring acts of the president as unconstitutional, and it can check the power of the legislative branch by declaring laws unconstitutional. This system may seem like it could cause inefficiency in the government, but it helps to maintain a healthy balance of power between the three branches.

Which of the following is the most likely conclusion that can be drawn based on the previous reading passage?

(A) The writers of the Constitution liked the number three.

(B) The writers of the Constitution wanted to make sure that the branches of government didn't share any powers, so they created three different branches of government.

(C) The writers of the Constitution made three branches of government share the powers of government so that one part of the government didn't become tyrannical and shut down the other parts of the government.

(D) The writers of the government gave each branch some power over the other two branches so one branch could never dominate the federal government.

Wait for me. I gotta go and sharpen my pencil—there was a lot of important stuff in that passage!

You're right, Chi. There was quite a bit of information in that passage. In addition, it was well organized and straightforward, as are most textbooks. These characteristics play right into the reader's hands, though. If you look at each one of the possible answer choices carefully, you will see that at first glance they all look like good choices, except for choice **(A)**. Choice **(B)** probably isn't correct, because the passage never talked about sharing particular powers. Choice **(C)** probably isn't correct, because there was no mention of tyranny or shutting down the other parts of the government. With the process of elimination, choice **(D)** seems right. Is it? Absolutely. Even though it doesn't say it word for word in the passage, all the facts of the passage support the conclusion made by choice **(D)**. Do you see how all your skills combined give you the ability to draw a conclusion?

Let's try another textbook passage. For all you non-history buffs out there, we'll change the topic for you.

> Ozone depletion has occurred because of human-induced activities. Ozone acts as a natural filter in the stratosphere, protecting life on Earth from overexposure to the sun's harmful ultraviolet radiation. However, the concentration of the ozone has become compromised by human use of harmful chemicals, and it has become a pollutant in the lower atmosphere. One group of chemicals, chlorofluorocarbons (CFCs), which are used in refrigerants, foam, solvents, and propellants, have caused "holes" or extremely depleted areas to appear in the ozone. Several international treaties have been signed to limit and eliminate the use and production of chlorofluorocarbons.

Which of the following is the most likely conclusion that can be drawn based on the previous reading passage?

(A) CFCs are dangerous enough that several countries have given serious thought to the potential harm that CFCs might cause to the atmosphere directly and to humans indirectly.

(B) CFCs should be banned in industrialized nations.

(C) The ozone layer should be restored as quickly as possible.

(D) The ozone layer may be responsible for allowing too much ultraviolet radiation to reach the Earth's surface.

That must be why Mr. Osgood, my science teacher, won't put hairspray on his toupée!

This passage, like the other passage, is chock full of good information and, like the other passage, is organized well. If you read through each of the possible answer choices, you should notice that all but one of them isn't supported too well by the previous passage. The correct answer is choice **(A)**. You definitely have the idea now, especially because this chapter is more or less a review of the previous chapter's strategies. The main difference is that a textbook passage will have more important facts and information than other reading passages. That means you will have a lot of information to handle when you have to answer recall questions and draw conclusions based on the same passage.

No sweat, man! Don't forget, you're talking to Chi!

Let's review briefly before you do a chapter review and then move on to a new concept:

- ★ Drawing conclusions from a textbook passage is based primarily on locating the important facts and information.
- ★ As you already know, you should read slowly and use your "writing stick" to help locate and identify that information.
- ★ As you read, develop a mental image of the big picture the passage is trying to paint for you.
- ★ Then, try to imagine the next logical step in the progression of the passage. With these pieces of information, you're more than ready to handle any question that requires you to draw a conclusion.

Get Wise!

Read the following passages, and answer the question that follows each.

1. Geography is the study of Earth's physical features and the way people have adapted to these physical features. Geography is concerned not only with physical geographic features but also with cultural geographic features. Physical geographic features include things such as land, water, mountains, and plains. Cultural geographic features include such things as human architecture or manmade changes to Earth's physical features. The science of geography can be divided into two branches, systematic and regional. Systematic geography deals with individual elements of Earth's physical and cultural features. Regional geography, on the other hand, deals with the physical and cultural features in a particular region, or area, of Earth's surface.

Which of the following is the most likely conclusion that can be drawn based on the previous reading passage?

(A) Geography is pretty simple because there are only four different things to study.

(B) Geographers have to know much, much more than states and capitals, rivers, and mountain ranges.

(C) The science of geography is a science that has been around for more than six thousand years.

(D) Geography is a relatively new science.

2. Elements are substances composed of atoms that have the same nuclear charges and electron configurations. As these elements were being discovered, there was a need for classification. Dmitry Mendeleyev was the first scientist to notice that elements can be ordered into families based on similar chemical and physical properties. He observed that properties of elements go through cycles, from elements with the lowest atomic weights to elements with the highest atomic weights. These cycles of properties were described as being **periodic**, meaning that they created patterns that affected how an element was grouped in the table. Improvements were later made to Mendeleyev's theory, particularly the discovery of the atomic number. The modern **periodic table of elements** now ranks elements according to the atomic number instead of the atomic weight. After further research, substantial evidence suggested that other properties of elements also vary periodically with the atomic number.

Which of the following is the most likely conclusion that can be drawn based on the previous reading passage?

(A) The elements that are known to people do not have some random order but rather can be classified in an organized manner.

(B) The elements on the periodic table are capable of producing nuclear energy.

(C) Mendeleyev was a brilliant man with incredible foresight.

(D) The periodic table may be obsolete once other more random elements are discovered.

How Wise?

1. **(B)** Geographers have to know much, much more than states and capitals, rivers, and mountain ranges.

2. **(A)** The elements that are known to man do not have some random order but rather can be classified in an organized manner.

Chapter 18

Everybody Has One

Surely, you've heard people say about opinions, "Everybody has one." Now you're really wondering what this chapter is about. You do realize, don't you, that many things that are written sound like facts but are nothing more than someone's opinion? In the realm of reading comprehension, being able to tell the difference between fact and opinion may mean the difference between nailing a reading passage and coming away from the passage with no idea what you just read.

You know I have an opinion about everything! And that's a fact!

When you're dealing with fact and opinion, you must be careful. Some people have a knack for stating an opinion and making it sound like the truth. You probably know someone who is really good at telling you what he or she thinks is the truth, and it sounds rock solid. Then, on the other hand, there are those people who can state facts, but they just don't sound credible. You know, some politicians, some infomercial spokespeople, some of your friends. The first trick to making the distinction between fact and opinion is simply knowing the difference between the two.

A fact is something that is known or proven or undeniable. For example, it is a fact that gravity causes dropped objects to fall to the ground. This is proven every time a bunch of cheerleaders drop the girl at the top of the pyramid and every time the centerfielder misplays a long fly ball. There is no debating the force of gravity. If you think something is a fact, ask yourself "Is it debatable?" If it's open for debate, it can't really be a fact, can it? An opinion, on the other hand, is something that is merely believed to be true. For example, many people claim that Duke has the best basketball team in the country. Although there is some evidence that may support this claim, this claim must be subjected to the question you learned earlier. "Is it debatable?" The answer, of course, is "yes." Therefore, the claim that Duke University has the best basketball team is merely an opinion.

Another important thing to understand is that fact and opinion can be cleverly interwoven in the same passage and even in the same sentence. Look at the following sentence:

> George Washington was not only the first president of the United States but also the most handsome president of the United States.

Oh, man, someone needs glasses!

Of course, the previous example is somewhat of a stretch, but it serves its purpose. There can be no debating that Washington was indeed the first president;

at least that's what was said in *Get Wise! Mastering U.S. History.* As for whether Washington was the most handsome president we've ever had, that is certainly up for debate. Be sure that you don't get fooled into thinking that everything in every sentence is either fact or opinion.

One more thing. You must be aware of where you are most likely to encounter fact and where you are most likely to encounter opinion. How about a textbook? Mostly facts there, but you might find opinions there, too. What about an academic journal? Almost entirely facts, but you may find an author's opinion or hypothesis. Newspaper? Lots of facts, but some opinions, too. Works of nonfiction? They should be full of facts, but you might find opinions, too. Do you see the pattern here? You can't pick up something to read and decide right away if it is mostly fact or mostly opinion. You have to read through it and decide for yourself if it is fact or opinion. Let's do a little exercise to help you get used to deciphering the fact/opinion code.

With each of the following statements, write "F" in the blank if the statement is fact and write "O" in the blank if the statement is opinion.

____ **1.** New York City is the largest city in the state of New York.

____ **2.** Chocolate pudding is the best dessert in the world.

____ **3.** I believe the fastest animal on Earth is the thoroughbred horse.

____ **4.** Winter in Wisconsin is definitely too cold.

____ **5.** Hockey is the roughest sport in North America.

____ **6.** Vitamins are important for the growth and development of bones.

____ **7.** Fast cars are not really dangerous, as long as the driver is capable of handling speed.

____ **8.** Money is the root of all evil.

____ **9.** Family portraits make the best presents.

____ **10.** Reading is important for people who want to be successful.

How about one that says, "Chi is the coolest chick around"?

The answers are as follows:

1. F
2. O
3. O
4. O
5. O
6. F
7. O
8. O
9. O
10. F

Let's put this exercise in the context of a reading passage. After all, that's where you'll need to decide what's fact and what's opinion. Read the following passage. As you read, **circle** any sentence that is a statement of fact and **underline** any sentence that is a statement of opinion.

> Watching movies is one of the biggest forms of entertainment in the United States today. Many people watch movies at theaters, whereas many people rent movies and watch them at home. People who watch movies at home watch practically all their movies on DVD nowadays. Nobody watches movies on VHS anymore. Comedies are probably the favorite choice of most people who watch movies for

entertainment. Besides comedies, there are other genres of movies available, including sci-fi, horror, action, and animated. Only geeks like animated movies, though. Movies are the perfect answer for what to do on a date, because everyone likes to see a movie on a date. Black-and-white movies are OK for dates but generally only appeal to old people. At theaters, popcorn and soft drinks are often available to moviegoers. However, everyone sneaks in candy and snacks from home.

Hey, I thought I was the only one who sneaked in snacks!

So, how many sentences did you circle and how many did you underline? You should have circled three sentences: the first, the sixth, and the tenth sentences. Every other sentence is merely the author's opinion. Here's a little something to remember—even if you agree with or believe a statement, it may still be an opinion and not a fact! Let's do one more reading passage just to make sure you're getting the hang of it. This passage is an excerpt of a newspaper article.

Uncle Jim's Barbecue will be celebrating its Grand Opening on Monday. To celebrate, Jim Cook, the owner, will have every item on the menu on sale. Cook also will offer discounts to senior citizens and police officers.

Uncle Jim's Barbecue boasts some 75 menu items, including brisket, ribs, sausage, burgers, steaks, chicken, onion rings, fries, and more. Jim's beverage selection is quite varied, too, with tea, lemonade, mineral

water, soft drinks, and more. The atmosphere at Uncle Jim's is intended to remind patrons of an Old West wagon train.

Uncle Jim's is located at 2517 South 33rd near downtown. Uncle Jim's is the best barbecue in the state, and it would be a mistake to miss out on this local treasure.

See, now I'm hungry again!

How did you do this time? Let's get right to it. The only sentence in the whole passage that should be underlined as opinion is the last sentence. Everything else in the passage can be verified, except for the last sentence. Even if you agree that Uncle Jim makes the best darn barbecue around, the statement is merely an opinion. Let's do a quick review of fact and opinion just to refresh your memory. Facts are any statements that are undeniable and can be proven without a doubt. Opinions, on the other hand, are statements of belief and cannot be proven. A good fact or opinion test is to ask of a given statement, "Is it debatable?" If the statement is debatable, the statement is opinion. Finally, any amount of facts can be mixed in with any amount of opinion, so you will have to take every sentence on a case-by-case basis. In some cases, you may need to judge entire passages as a statement of fact or statement of opinion.

I do believe I can do this, and that's a fact, Jack!

Get Wise

Read the following passage. As you read, **circle** the sentences that are statements of fact and **underline** the sentences that are statements of opinion.

> Dogs and cats are both common house pets in America. What many people don't realize is that pot-bellied pigs are the best animals a person can buy for a pet. It's true that dogs and cats can be house trained. However, pot-bellied pigs are much more lovable and cuddly than dogs and cats. Additionally, the pigs are much cuter than dogs or cats. A person trying to find the perfect pet should simply look no further than the local pot-bellied pig farm. Kids love pot-bellied pigs, and these pigs all love kids. Some dogs and cats have been known to bite or scratch. Pot-bellied pigs are just too cute to ever do something like that. Because dogs and cats are so common, guys can attract girls much easier with a pot-bellied pig on the end of a leash. Pot-bellied pigs just can't be beat as pets.

How Wise?

The first, third, and eighth sentences should be circled, and the rest of the sentences should be underlined.

Chapter 19

That's a Wrap

When we say, "That's a Wrap," we didn't mean that we were wrapping up the whole book. We're just going to wrap up the section on reading comprehension. We've taken just about every angle there is to take with reading comprehension, and you're ready to move on to some more advanced skills. Before we do, though, let's quickly review the skills you've been practicing the last several chapters.

One important skill involved in comprehension is predicting the outcome or ending of a reading passage. Here are a few pointers to help you figure out how a passage will end:

- ★ As you read, identify the important information in the passage.
- ★ Using the important information in the passage, try to picture the story or events in your imagination.
- ★ Use the order in which the events or facts are presented to visualize the natural or logical progression.

- ★ Based on the order of the events or facts, make a logical conclusion about how the passage is most likely to end.
- ★ Think of the passage as a puzzle, and try to imagine what the last piece of the puzzle will look like.
- ★ When all else fails, tie a bandanna around your head and find a crystal ball.

I get it! A fortune-teller, right! Very funny!

The next skill we worked on was drawing conclusions. Remember that this skill is similar to a skill that a detective might use. Here are some tips for successfully drawing conclusions from a reading passage:

- ★ Just like when you're predicting the outcome of a passage, identify the important information and facts within the passage.
- ★ As you read, try to see a pattern or figure out the likely outcome of the progression of the passage.
- ★ Use the conclusion-drawing skills you use every day to make a conclusion based on the pattern of the facts in the passage.
- ★ When drawing a conclusion from a textbook, read the passage at a slower pace and pay extra attention to the facts, figures, and important information in the passage; textbooks obviously contain many more facts than your average reading passage.

I can safely conclude that I know how to do this now!

Next we looked at facts and opinions. Remember that if you are trying to gather facts and important information, you have to know the difference between fact and opinion. If you wanted to get some insight into what an author thinks or believes, then opinion would be fine. However, if something that seems factual but is merely an opinion, you could easily be misled. Here are some things to keep in mind about fact and opinion.

- ★ A fact is anything that is undeniable, irrefutable, or able to be proven.
- ★ An opinion is anything that is believed to be true.
- ★ To determine if something is fact or opinion, ask the question, "Is it debatable?"
- ★ Fact and opinion are often included in the same reading passage, so it is important not to assume that an entire passage is not factual.
- ★ Also, because fact and opinion can be included in the same reading passage, it is just as important to not write off an entire passage as opinion.

The fact is everybody has an opinion!

The last part of comprehension that we covered was dealing with emotional arguments and rational, logical arguments. We're going to be rational about this, and we're going to try not to get wrapped up in emotions as we refresh your memory about emotional and rational statements. Here's the scoop.

- ★ Rational, logical statements are those that are based on facts.
- ★ Emotional statements are those that are based on what someone believes or feels.
- ★ Emotional statements that are based somewhat on facts are still not trustworthy, because they are usually tainted by the author's personal beliefs.

Before we move on to some totally new ideas and concepts that will require you to use all your comprehension skills together, let's do some practice exercises that will test your ability to use all the skills we reviewed in this chapter.

Get Wise!

Read the following passages, and answer the questions that follow each. Remember to pay attention to the details, facts, or events in each passage and try to envision the passage as you read.

> The Lakers are the greatest basketball team ever. They play in the coolest city, Los Angeles, and they have the best team colors, purple and gold. The other teams in the league are terrible compared to the Lakers. The Lakers also have the best atmosphere for games. Going to Lakers games is the coolest thing to do. All the seats are great seats, and all the fans are friendly and helpful. The Lakers win more than any other team, and they have the best players and the best coach. The players are friendly, because they will stop and talk to the fans after the game. They even sign autographs when they have time. The coach is also the greatest coach in the league, because he knows everything about basketball. He should write books about basketball if he hasn't already. No other coach in the league knows as much about basketball as he does. There aren't even any other sports teams as cool as the Lakers, and the other sports teams can't be as much fun to watch in person! The Lakers rock!

1. Which of the following conclusions can be made based on the previous passage?

(A) The author has attended a game at every NBA arena in the country.

(B) The author knows each of the players and the coach personally.

(C) The author has attended Lakers games.

(D) The author is an NBA player.

2. Which of the following statements is based on fact rather than opinion?

(A) The Lakers are the greatest basketball team ever.

(B) They play in the coolest city, Los Angeles, and they have the best team colors, purple and gold.

(C) The Lakers also have the best atmosphere for games.

(D) None of the above sentences is based on fact.

3. Which of the following can be said of the previous passage?

(A) The passage is entirely emotional.

(B) The passage is entirely logical.

(C) The passage is mostly emotional.

(D) The passage is mostly logical.

The most annoying thing in the world is getting ridiculous spam e-mails. Nobody ever reads those things anyway! Besides, who sits around and makes those things up? Those people must be crazy! The e-mails I get range from offers for refinancing mortgages to get-rich-quick schemes to psychic readings to investment strategies to art school to ancient treasure maps to free cash to hair-loss prevention. It seems like my e-mail inbox gets ten spam e-mails every day. The *Journal of Internet Studies* says that of all spam e-mails, only 3 percent of them ever get a response. That percentage is too small to be worth anybody's time and effort! There must be fifty zillion e-mail addresses in the world, and somebody somewhere has decided to drive every one of the e-mail address owners insane by sending them all spam! There must be some way to stop all the madness, but I haven't figured it out yet. Spam writers must be either the loneliest people in the world or just the most persistent people in the world.

4. Which of the following conclusions can be made based on the previous passage?

(A) The author spends a relatively large amount of time sending and receiving e-mails.

(B) The author has never used a computer.

(C) The author has tried the offers and has been disappointed in the results.

(D) The author wants to get into the spam business but doesn't know where to start.

5. Which of the following statements is based on fact rather than on opinion?

(A) Spam writers must be either the loneliest people in the world or just the most persistent people in the world.

(B) The most annoying thing in the world is getting ridiculous spam e-mails.

(C) The *Journal of Internet Studies* says that of all spam e-mails, only 3 percent of them ever get a response.

(D) It seems like my e-mail inbox gets ten spam e-mails every day.

6. Which of the following can be said of the passage above?

(A) The passage is entirely emotional.

(B) The passage is entirely logical.

(C) The passage is mostly emotional.

(D) The passage is mostly logical.

How Wise?

1. (C) The author has attended Lakers games.

2. (D) None of the above sentences is based on fact.

3. (A) The passage is entirely emotional.

4. (A) The author spends a relatively large amount of time sending and receiving e-mails.

5. (C) The *Journal of Internet Studies* says that of all spam e-mails, only 3 percent of them ever get a response.

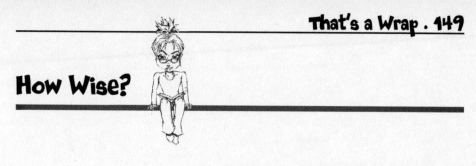

6. (C) The passage is mostly emotional.

chapter 20

That's the Dumbest ...

Have you ever tried to have a serious debate with somebody and the other person just ranted on and on about nothing instead of discussing the facts? Or maybe you tried talking to your little sister about *not* borrowing your clothes without asking and why that's a problem for you. Your sister, on the other hand, called you a selfish bully, accused you of being tyrannical, said you have bad breath, and then launched into a tirade about how insensitive you are. Sometimes, authors use arguments to make a point about one thing or another. These arguments can be based on facts and figures or these arguments can be based on nothing at all. Logical, reasonable, and rational arguments are based on facts. When authors base an argument on nothing more than their own beliefs, the argument tends to be emotional. Let's look at a few examples so you can see the difference between the two.

People are always accusing me of being too emotional. I mean, how irrational is that?

To the editor:
Our old friend Mr. Cartwright has thrown his hat in the ring again for the office of President of the Southwest Chapter of Bottlecap Collectors. Mr. Cartwright is a three-time loser who has never won anything worthwhile in his life. He doesn't know anything about holding office. He doesn't have any idea how to be a leader, and he doesn't set a good example for others. Mr. Cartwright is only interested in his own career, and he has no regard for the feelings of others. Mr. Cartwright will lie, cheat, and steal if it gives him a better chance of finally being elected to an office that he simply has no business holding. Mr. Cartwright is the wrong guy for the job, and he doesn't deserve a single vote.

I. M. Wright
Lenox Drive

Now read this one:

> **To the editor:**
> **Mr. Cartwright, who has unsuccessfully run for the office of President of the Southwest Chapter of Bottlecap Collectors, is seeking election once again. Mr. Cartwright has never been elected to a leadership position before and has never attended a leadership conference. In addition, Mr. Cartwright has only been collecting bottlecaps for three years. He has never won any awards, such as Collector of the Year or Bottlecap Bossman. Mr. Cartwright's legal record indicates that he has been arrested four times for stealing bottlecaps from the soda bottles in our local grocery store! Based on his record, Mr. Cartwright does not appear to be the ideal candidate for such an esteemed position.**
>
> **N. V. Wrong**
> **Carnegie Drive**

The two passages are obviously very different. One is based on facts, or information that can be proven, and the other is based on emotional arguments. Which of the passages seems the more credible to you? Obviously, if you want to make a rational decision about something you should have rational information. Doesn't the first passage remind you of a political candidate just trying to run his opponent into the ground with a mudslinging campaign? You must be able to recognize the difference between an emotional argument and a rational argument. Standardized tests, though, aren't going to give you two passages and then ask you to know the difference between the two. Let's take a look at a passage that has a mixture of rational and emotional arguments. After you read the passage, answer the question that follows.

So, there. I *can* be emotional and rational at the same time. But really, who wants to be rational? Hey, that would make a great game show! I could be Regis!

Jake's Cakes

If you want to buy a cake in this town, you have to buy it at Jake's Cakes. Jake's Cakes is the best bakery in town, and Jake is the greatest cook who has ever worked in this town. Jake graduated at the top of his class at the Culinary Academy of South Dakota where he majored in cake baking. He has a natural ability to get the best out of flour and milk and eggs. Jake is better than any of those stuffy old cooks on TV. In fact, Jake should have his own show because he knows more than they do! Those other bakeries in town aren't worth a flip! Jake publishes his prices and his prices are the lowest in town. Nobody bakes with as much passion as Jake, so you have to buy from him! Jake is also the cutest baker in town and probably in the state. He's a genius when it comes to cakes, so anyone who wants a good cake has to go see Jake!

Which of the following is a statement that makes a logical, rather than an emotional, argument?

(A) He has a natural ability to get the best out of flour and milk and eggs.

(B) If you want to buy a cake in this town, you have to buy it at Jake's Cakes.

(C) Nobody in town bakes with as much passion as Jake, so you have to buy from him!

(D) Jake graduated at the top of his class at the Culinary Academy of South Dakota, where he majored in cake baking.

Here we go again, making me hungry with all this talk about food!

Before you go, Chi, which statement can be verified as fact? Using your skills from the last chapter, you should have selected choice **(D)**. Even though choices **(A)** and **(B)** aren't as emotionally charged as choice **(C)**, they are still opinion-based arguments. When you're looking for solid information, you can't rely on someone's opinions and emotionally based arguments. Now granted, some of your closest friends may have a hard time making a rational argument, but they can still base a statement on fact.

One of the most common places you'll need to be able to distinguish the difference between emotional and rational arguments is in the advertising that you see and hear every day. You see commercials all the time that make promises. You read print ads promising everything from weight loss to clear skin to whiter teeth to hair growing back in bald spots. What's the real deal and what's bogus? Let's look at an example of an ad.

How many times have you made a New Year's resolution to lose weight only to forget about it a few weeks later?

I was guilty of this myself but then I heard about *Slim-Up Juice* and thought, why should I wait until January 1st to make a change for the better? I started drinking a pint of *Slim-Up Juice* twice a day and saw results almost immediately! For those of you who have broken your New Year's resolution to lose weight, it is not too late to start over, and this is the perfect diet solution for you! With *Slim-Up Juice* and a little exercise, you'll be ready for summer days on the beach! What are you waiting for?

Call 1-888-SLIM-UP NOW!

It worked for me, and it can work for you!

I bet that juice is the kind that makes the bathroom your second home! Been there, done that.

Where are the facts? Where is the evidence? Where are the rational statements? There aren't any! This whole paragraph is one big emotional appeal to the reader.

By now you get the idea. Rational arguments are the only ones from which you can draw reliable information because they're based on facts. Emotional arguments aren't reliable because they aren't based on facts and they are tainted by emotions. Let's put all this together and practice with the following reading passage.

Get Wise!

Read the following passage and answer the questions that follow.

Big Daddy Bill E Bob has to be the worst musician to come along in years! He should have known that country music doesn't mix with hip-hop. Belt buckles and bling bling just don't go together like boots and buckles. Big Daddy Bill E Bob, according to the *Weekly Chart Watcher* magazine, has only sold 502 CDs to date. Nobody wants to listen to a guy bust rhymes about pickups, trains, and his dog! Big Daddy Bill E Bob's videos are terrible, too. Big Daddy decked out in a cowboy hat, a big belt buckle, and snakeskin boots just doesn't belong in the same picture as a chromed-out low rider with 20-inch rims. People really shouldn't buy his CDs or go to his concerts because he just isn't any good at what he does. He can't possibly be serious!

1. Which of the following statements is the only statement that can be accepted as factual?

(A) Big Daddy Bill E Bob has to be the worst musician to come along in years!

(B) Big Daddy Bill E Bob, according to the *Weekly Chart Watcher* magazine, has only sold 502 CDs to date.

(C) Nobody wants to listen to a guy bust rhymes about pickups, trains, and his dog!

(D) He can't possibly be serious!

2. Overall, the passage above is best classified as which of the following?

(A) Entirely emotional

(B) Entirely rational

(C) Mostly emotional

(D) Mostly rational

How Wise?

1. **(B)** Big Daddy Bill E Bob, according to the Weekly Chart Watcher magazine, has only sold 502 CDs to date.

2. **(C)** Mostly emotional

Puzzle 3

Complete the following puzzle using the words you learned in Chapters 14–20. Puzzle solutions are in the back of the book.

Across

3. NOT AN ASSUMPTION; BASED ON FACTS
6. ARGUMENTS BASED ON FACTS AND RATIONALE
7. TO FIND THE IMPLIED IDEA, READ ____ THE LINES
9. ARGUMENTS NOT BASED ON FACTS

Down

1. FORTUNE-TELLING DEVICE NOT PERMITTED ON STANDARDIZED TESTS
2. OPPOSITE OF OPINION; PROVABLE
4. HINTED AT OR SUGGESTED, BUT NOT WRITTEN OUT
5. TO MAKE AN EDUCATED GUESS ABOUT AN OUTCOME
8. YOU MUST IDENTIFY MOST IMPORTANT INFO AND FOLLOW LOGICAL PROGRESSION TO PREDICT OUTCOMES IN THESE
10. EVERYBODY HAS ONE

chapter 21

A Comprehensive Review

Let's do a complete review exercise covering all the comprehension skills you've learned so far. If there are any skills you are unsure about, refer to the appropriate chapter. Once you are ready, gather your reading tools, find a quiet place to work, and do the review. Don't forget that anything goes with these reading passages. Here we go!

Get Wise!

Although a child's sleep patterns may change periodically, it is still important for a child to have a bedtime routine. For some toddlers, a trip to the bathroom for a bath, to brush teeth, and to use the potty is a great way to signal bedtime. For others, a couple of good books and a song send them off to lullaby land. It is important to remember, though, that a really upbeat song may not be the best choice. Also, stories with giants, monsters, ghosts, ghouls, goblins, trolls, and witches probably aren't the best choices for bedtime stories. Another good bedtime tip is to avoid letting a child have a glass of water before bed. Worse than a glass of water, though, would be soda and candy before bedtime. The substance of the routine is less important than the fact of the routine and the consistency in following it.

1. Which of the following is the best title for the previous passage?
   - **(A)** "Ten Ways to Get Good Sleep"
   - **(B)** "The Best Bedtime Routine for Children"
   - **(C)** "The Importance of a Bedtime Routine"
   - **(D)** "Some Bedtime Routine Ideas"

2. Which of the following is the main idea of the previous passage?
   - **(A)** Although a child's sleep patterns may change periodically, it is still important for a child to have a bedtime routine.
   - **(B)** The substance of the routine is less important than the fact of the routine and the consistency in following it.
   - **(C)** For some toddlers, a trip to the bathroom for a bath, to brush teeth, and to use the potty is a great way to signal bedtime.
   - **(D)** For others, a couple of good books and a song send them off to lullaby land.

3. Which of the following conclusions can be drawn based on the information in the previous passage?
   - **(A)** Children don't sleep well if they haven't had a busy night.
   - **(B)** Toddlers don't sleep as well as older children.
   - **(C)** By keeping a child in a nighttime routine, the entire family is much more likely to enjoy a restful night's sleep.
   - **(D)** Sleep patterns vary according to how the parents put the child to sleep.

4. Based on the information in the passage, which of the following is fine for a child to have before bedtime?

(A) A glass of water

(B) A soda

(C) Candy

(D) A bath

A common problem for kids is chewing gum getting stuck in their hair. Sometimes kids get gum stuck in their own hair. Sometimes, though, kids get gum stuck in other kids' hair. Regardless of how gum gets in a kid's hair, the kid and the parents have a sticky situation on their hands. One of the oldest tricks in the book is smearing peanut butter in the hair to make the gum less sticky and easier to pull out of the hair. Another great trick is rubbing ice in the kid's hair. Somehow, the ice makes it easier to get the gum out of the hair. Beware of the old wives' tales, though. Mayonnaise, pickle juice, motor oil, hair spray, WD-40, hot sauce, buttermilk, and seawater do not do anything but make the mess bigger. When all else fails, use scissors to carefully cut the gum out of the hair.

5. Which of the following is the main idea of the previous passage?

(A) A common problem for kids is chewing gum getting stuck in hair.

(B) Beware of the old wives' tales, though.

(C) When all else fails, use scissors to carefully cut the gum out of the hair.

(D) The implied main idea is, "Although chewing gum in a kid's hair can be a big mess, there are several ways to get the gum out."

6. Which of the following is *not* a way to get gum out of hair?
   (A) Peanut butter
   (B) Ice
   (C) Hair spray
   (D) Scissors

A set of imaginary vertical lines divides the earth into 24 geographic regions. These regions are known as time zones. Each zone represents 1 hour of the day and measures a distance of approximately 15 degrees across. All clocks within the same time zone should be set to the same time and, generally, are 1 hour later than those of the time zone to the immediate west. The 0 degrees longitude line, known as the Prime Meridian, runs north and south through the Royal Greenwich Observatory in Greenwich, England. Each of the 12 time zones to the west of the Prime Meridian decrease in time by 1 hour, whereas each of the time zones to the east of the Prime Meridian increase in time by 1 hour. The International Date Line lies on the opposite side of the world from the Prime Meridian and is located at 180 degrees longitude. The time zones on each side of the Date Line are in different days. If a person crosses the International Date Line heading west, he or she will lose a day; if a person crosses the International Date Line heading east, he or she will gain a day.

7. According to the previous passage, the earth is covered by how many time zones?
   (A) 12
   (B) 24
   (C) 180
   (D) 0

8. Which of the following would be the best title for the previous passage?

(A) "24 Hours a Day and 7 Days a Week"

(B) "From Greenwich to the Line and Back Again"

(C) "The Earth's Time Zones"

(D) "International Dating Has Never Been So Easy"

Memo

To: All Bag Boys at Harvest House Grocery Store

From time to time we all need to be reminded that customer service is our number-one priority here at Harvest House. First, never pack frozen foods in the same grocery bags as hot meals, rotisserie chickens, or fresh-baked garlic bread. Second, don't pack eggs and bread in the same grocery bag as heavy items, such as cans and jars. Third, don't put more than 1 gallon of milk or 2 two-liter bottles or 2 three-liter bottles in the same bag. Customers don't really appreciate grocery bags tearing open and heavy bottles falling out onto their toes. Third, don't comment on customers' purchases as you are bagging or carrying. For example, comments like "Why did you decide to put the breath mints back?" are just not appropriate. Likewise, comments such as "Are you sure you really want all those chocolate bars?" and "What kind of rash did you buy that medicine for?" just have to stop. Finally, please don't ask the customers for tips after you bag the items.

9. Which of the following is the most important suggestion made by the author of the memo?

(A) Never pack frozen foods in the same grocery bags as hot meals, rotisserie chickens, or fresh-baked garlic bread.

(B) Don't pack eggs and bread in the same grocery bag as heavy items, such as cans and jars.

(C) Don't comment on customers' purchases as you are bagging or carrying.

(D) Please don't ask the customers for tips after you bag the items.

10. Which of the following is most likely the main idea of the previous passage?

(A) Customers at Harvest House Grocery Store are picky.

(B) Employees of Harvest House Grocery Store must be concerned first and foremost with customer service and politeness.

(C) Harvest House Grocery Store has rude employees.

(D) Harvest House Grocery Store has curious employees.

11. Which of the following conclusions can be drawn based on the information in the previous passage?

(A) Harvest House Grocery Store employees are always the most considerate employees in town.

(B) Harvest House Grocery Store employees have not been committed to customer service in the past.

(C) Customers have been appreciative of the polite manner in which Harvest House Grocery Store employees have acted.

(D) Customers too often leave without tipping employees even when the employees do a great job.

Dear Editor,

It would appear that schools within our county are advocating the use of electric pencil sharpeners in the classroom. I am shocked and appalled by such advocacy. The school board obviously has not given any thought to the grave consequences of the use of electric pencil sharpeners. First and foremost, electric pencil sharpeners encourage wastefulness and thereby encourage the needless destruction of thousands and thousands of acres of rain forests. Second, pencils made of real wood have feelings and are sensitive to the cruel grinding and crushing action of the electric pencil sharpeners. Insensitive kids may be tempted to grind the poor, helpless pencils down to nothing more than nubs, with total disregard for the feelings of the pencils. We must do something to stop the unnecessary destruction of these poor little guys! A boycott of electric pencil sharpeners and wooden pencils will help slow the destruction of the world's rain forests.

Sincerely,
Ima Treehugger

12. Which of the following sentences is based on fact rather than on opinion in the previous passage?

(A) It would appear that schools within our county are advocating the use of electric pencil sharpeners in the classroom.

(B) First and foremost, electric pencil sharpeners encourage wastefulness and thereby encourage the needless destruction of thousands and thousands of acres of rain forests.

(C) A boycott of electric pencil sharpeners and wooden pencils will help slow the destruction of the world's rain forests.

(D) All of the sentences in the previous passage are based on opinion rather than on fact.

13. Which of the following best characterizes the previous passage?

(A) The passage is based entirely on emotional arguments.

(B) The passage is based entirely on logical arguments.

(C) The passage is based mostly on emotional arguments.

(D) The passage is based partly on emotional arguments.

Matt and Marty were really bored one day, so they thought they would think of something really exciting to do. Matt suggested that the two take Marty's mother's station wagon into the woods for some mudding. Marty balked at the idea, because he feared he would get the car stuck in the mud because it wasn't equipped for mudding. Marty explained that the station wagon didn't have four-wheel drive or mud tires. In addition, Marty pointed out that he didn't have a cell phone or a walkie-talkie in case something happened. However, the sky was finally clear, and the boys had been dying to get outside and do something. The lure of the beautiful weather was just too much. Matt pleaded his case, and Marty finally gave in to temptation. Marty grabbed the keys and headed out the door. The two adventurous boys drove out to the country and found a nice trail leading off the highway. They both yelled like the Dukes of Hazzard as they barreled into the mud slick that lay ahead of them.

14. Which of the following is implied in the previous passage?

(A) The weather finally cleared up after a period of rainy weather.

(B) Neither Matt nor Marty knew how to drive.

(C) Only Marty had a driver's license.

(D) Matt and Marty had been on restriction or had been grounded.

15. Which of the following is the most likely outcome of the previous passage?

(A) Matt and Marty change their minds and return the car to the driveway.

(B) Matt and Marty get the car stuck in the mud and call for help.

(C) Matt and Marty get the car stuck in the mud and have to walk back to the highway to get help.

(D) Matt and Marty go mudding and have a great time.

How Wise?

1. (D) "Some Bedtime Routine Ideas"

2. (A) Although a child's sleep patterns may change periodically, it is still important for a child to have a bedtime routine.

3. (C) By keeping a child in a nighttime routine, the entire family is much more likely to enjoy a restful night's sleep.

4. (D) A bath

5. (D) The implied main idea is, "Although chewing gum in a kid's hair can be a big mess, there are several ways to get the gum out."

6. (C) Hair spray

7. (B) 24

8. (C) "The Earth's Time Zones"

9. (A) Never pack frozen foods in the same grocery bags as hot meals, rotisserie chickens, or fresh-baked garlic bread.

10. (B) Employees of Harvest House Grocery Store must be concerned first and foremost with customer service and politeness.

11. (B) Harvest House Grocery Store employees have not been committed to customer service in the past.

12. (D) All of the sentences in the previous passage are based on opinion rather than on fact.

13. (A) The passage is based entirely on emotional arguments.

14. (A) The weather finally cleared up after a period of rainy weather.

15. (C) Matt and Marty get the car stuck in the mud and have to walk back to the highway to get help.

chapter 22

Lit 101

Before we get into the rest of this chapter, read the following passage:

> As Marge climbed the ladder, she reflected on the storm that had shaken her to her very foundation. With each step upward, Marge began to distance herself from the stormy weather that had so affected her inner being and true soul. The closer Marge got to the top of the ladder, the brighter her surroundings grew. It was as if there were some powerful force or energy that surrounded her and engulfed her in a glaring but gentle shower of light. She carefully stepped off the ladder and floated back to the bottom from where she started her magnificent journey. Marge repeated the process over and over for a hundred lifetimes. Each time was exactly the same as before, but, strangely, Marge felt as if each time was

a new experience. After what must have been ten thousand journeys, Marge realized that she had been hearing voices, familiar voices. She couldn't understand what the voices were saying, if they were indeed saying anything at all, but they were oddly soothing.

What the heck was that?

Good question, Chi. What was that? You may have said to yourself, "Great! Now I have to read literature!" If that's what you were thinking, then you're absolutely right. However, if you think that garbage is what literature is all about, then you have another think coming. By the way, that passage was made up to prove a point. You know, just because something is called "literature" doesn't mean it is going to be whacked out like that stuff you just read or boring or any other stereotypical characteristic of literature. Now, here's something else to think about for a minute. Imagine, if you will, that you did read that crazy stuff in a literature book in class. First, you can bet that some people would call it a work of pure genius, whereas others would call it pure nonsense. Now imagine that your teacher is one of those people who thinks that he or she has some profound insight into every piece of literature ever written. Do you want someone else telling you what the literature means, or would you rather read it and decide for yourself? Of course you'd rather make up your own mind! Seriously, you don't want someone telling you that he or she totally understood that passage you read on the first page of this chapter and that it symbolizes the author's coming to grips with the loss of his guinea pig when he was seven years old.

Did anybody else notice that the answers in Chapter 21 *weren't* upside down? What's up (or upside down) with that?

Whatever, Chi! Many people cringe when they hear the word "literature," but there's no reason for you to cringe. Literature isn't necessarily written in some secret code or by an author in a drug-induced delirium state. The reason so many people don't want anything to do with literature is because they don't know how to read it. These same people probably don't even know what literature is.

Literature is stuffy old stuff written by stuffy old men and women who have been dead for at least 100 years!

Not exactly, Chi. First, literature isn't limited to a time period. Literature may be on the most recent bestseller list or it may be from ancient Greece. Generally speaking, literature includes novels, short stories, plays, and poems. We could write books and books on how to read and interpret literature. However, there are a few basic things you must know how to do as you read literature, and we're going to show you those things. There are no codes to crack, no secrets to discover, and no foreign language to learn. There are just a few basic skills to hone, and you'll be ready to jump right into whatever literature you want to try.

When you're reading a work of literature, especially if you are going to be tested on it, there are a few things you have to master. For example, you'll need to identify the theme of a piece of literature. You'll need to recognize an author's point of view. You'll need to recognize first-, second-, and third-person writing. You'll need to recognize when an author uses symbolism to make his or her writing more creative or interesting. You'll need to identify examples of personification. If you don't know what these things are, don't sweat it! We're going to show you everything you need to know!

I know all this stuff already! But, I guess I can review it a little. OK, you got me! I don't know what the heck you're talking about!

Thanks for being honest, Chi. Let's begin with something that's similar to some skills you've already developed. We're going to start with theme. The theme is sort of the cousin of the main idea and sort of the cousin of the topic or subject. The theme of a reading passage is not just what the passage is about; that would make the theme the subject or topic. Rather, the theme is what is said about the subject. Let's look at an example—it will be much easier to comprehend if you see a good example.

> Johnny believed he was the luckiest guy in the whole world. For 7 days straight, Johnny found a penny facing heads up. During the 7-day stretch, Johnny won a radio call-in contest on three different radio stations. Johnny hit a hole-in-one twice, once at a country club course and the other at a miniature-golf course. Johnny had three dates with the hottest girl in school during the 7-day period. Johnny was living the high life, and he was enjoying every minute of it. Then, Johnny woke up late on the eighth day. The electricity had gone out, and the digital alarm clock was flashing 12:00. Johnny got to school late and realized that his physics class had already left for its field trip to the amusement park. Johnny spent the rest of the day sitting in the school office doing his algebra homework. Johnny's good luck had run out.

Which of the following is the theme of the previous passage?

(A) Luck is all you need.

(B) Everybody is lucky.

(C) Some guys have all the luck.

(D) Luck is not consistent.

Let's start with the topic or the subject. You probably figured out quickly that the topic or subject of the passage is luck. After all, the whole passage is, in one form or another, about luck. So what did the passage say about luck? First, the passage discusses how lucky Johnny was for a while. Then, the passage explains that Johnny's luck changed. The passage doesn't just come right out and tell you, "My theme is blah blah blah." That would be too darn easy, don't you think? Several chapters back, you learned how to read between the lines and how to find the implied main idea. If you use those two skills, you can figure out the theme of this passage. Remember that the theme of a passage is not the topic but rather what the passage says about the topic. That eliminates choice **(A)**. The passage doesn't address luck as it pertains to everyone, so it can't be choice **(B)**. Choice **(C)** can't be right, because Johnny's luck ran out, so he doesn't have all the luck. That leaves choice **(D)**. The passage implies that Johnny was pretty lucky for a while, but then he was no longer lucky. With that in mind, it makes a lot of sense that the passage is explaining that luck will run out or, in other words, luck is not consistent. Therefore, the correct answer is **(D)**.

That's not so hard! I just used all the stuff I already learned! Piece of cake!

Great work! Here is something important you need to understand about theme. You may be asked to find the theme of a short reading passage, a short poem, a reading passage that is several pages long, or, perhaps in your lit class, an entire chapter or even an entire book. You really have to see the big picture to pick up the theme of a reading passage. Don't forget, finding the theme is similar to finding the main idea and the topic or subject. You've already practiced those skills, so it isn't much of a stretch to find the theme. Let's look at one more practice reading passage to make sure you get the hang of theme before we wrap up this chapter with a chapter review.

Dr. Jones always knew that happy patients healed more quickly than patients who were down or depressed. Therefore, Dr. Jones abandoned his traditional white coat and adopted a red clown nose and purple hair. Instead of Armani shoes, Dr. Jones wore giant red clown shoes. Dr. Jones believed that he could do more good with this unorthodox method of treatment than with the traditional by-the-book methods he learned in medical school. Dr. Jones, or "Doc" as his patients call him, was so passionate about his therapy that he funded several studies on the subject of laughter and its healing powers. The results of the study confirmed what Doc knew all along: laughter is the best medicine. Doc documented his more amazing cases in his journal and has made plans to publish a book on his greatest success stories. Doc created the Chuckles Foundation through which he made contact with other doctors who had come to the same realization. Hundreds of doctors contacted Doc and shared their success stories, too. Doc devoted his professional life to making patients smile and laugh and, therefore, get well. Every day, Doc's crazy antics contributed to the soothing and healing of his patients.

Which of the following is the theme of the previous passage?

(A) Laughter

(B) Laughter has healing powers.

(C) Doctors

(D) Doctors dress as clowns.

I had a funny doctor once. Of course, he had eyebrows that looked like caterpillars, so he wasn't being funny on purpose!

Laughter, by itself, really isn't the underlying theme, but it is a part of it. The use of laughter as a form of treatment is really what the passage addresses, but the author tells of the use of laughter through Doc. See how you have to read between the lines? If you picked up on all of these things, you probably also selected the correct answer, choice **(B)**. Use all your skills and find the themes in this chapter review before we move on to a new chapter.

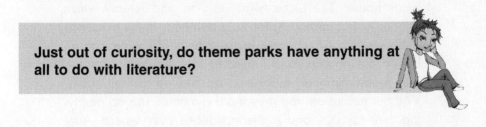

Just out of curiosity, do theme parks have anything at all to do with literature?

Get Wise!

Read the following passages and answer the questions that follow.

Amy approached the large, gray house with trepidation. She had done this before a thousand times but never at the Lucas house. The Lucas twins, Jerome and Jeremy, were famous, if not infamous, for their behavior in the presence of baby-sitters. Amy bravely entered the house, waved good-bye to the parents, and turned to face the twins. Jerome and Jeremy grinned evilly and dashed off to their room. Without hesitation, the 4-year-old dynamos started emptying their toy box and scattering debris everywhere. Amy rolled up her sleeves and charged into the fray. Twice Amy sustained small head wounds from flying building blocks. When Amy reached the toy box, the twins said they were hungry, and they rushed into the kitchen. Amy ran behind them and cut them off before they made it to the refrigerator. Amy scooped them up in a daring pass and buckled them into their booster seats all in one fell swoop. Amy heated the spaghetti while she kept an eye on the two monsters. She carefully made her way toward the table with the bowls of spaghetti. Amy scarcely had set down the spaghetti before the twins covered each other, and Amy, from head to toe with pasta and pasta sauce. Amy's boiling point was fast approaching. After dinner, Amy took them into the bathroom and bathed them. Before she could get the twins dry, though, they sprinted into their parents' bedroom and rolled around on the expensive imported silk bedspread. Amy grabbed the twins off the bed, put them in their pajamas, and sat them on the sofa in front of the TV. Minutes later, the parents returned, paid Amy her combat pay, and begged her to come back again the following weekend. Amy politely declined and ran to her car as fast as she could.

1. Which of the following is the theme of the previous passage?
   - **(A)** Baby-sitting
   - **(B)** Children
   - **(C)** Baby-sitting can be adventurous.
   - **(D)** Children can be lots of fun.

Mama Mia's Pizzeria has taken the art of pizza construction to new heights. In 1877, the original Mama Mia wrote a pizza-making manual for future generations of Mama Mia Pizzeria owners. Presentation, wrote Mama, is as important as flavor and aroma. Mama went on to say that the best pizzas are built in a particular manner. Sauce must always be spread liberally but evenly across the doughy crust. The next layer must be cheese. The cheese, as Mama explained, serves not only as a gooey, sticky place for toppings to hold onto, but also as a beautiful backdrop for the succulent vegetables and meat toppings. On the cheese, Mama wrote, must be the meats first, then peppers, then mushrooms and onions, and then any other desired toppings. Finally, Mama said, the top layer of cheese lies on top of the pizza to provide a cohesive outer shell. A pizza made any other way, Mama believed, was a travesty.

2. Which of the following is the theme of the previous passage?
   - **(A)** Pizzas
   - **(B)** Pizza-making
   - **(C)** Mama Mia was a progressive thinker.
   - **(D)** Pizza-making is an art.

How Wise?

1. (C) Baby-sitting can be adventurous.

2. (D) Pizza-making is an art.

chapter 23

Roses are Red, or Lit 102

Finding the theme in prose, or any literature that isn't poetry, is common in classrooms and on standardized tests. However, teachers and test-writers love to make students find the theme in poetry, too. Therefore, we're going to look at some poetry.

Hey, how about this: Roses are red. Violets are blue. I hate poetry. How 'bout you?

Now, Chi, how much poetry have you really read? You know, there's a lot more poetry out there than just the sappy love poems that the nerd in the back of the class writes to the cheerleaders! In fact, there are probably more different types of poetry than prose. For example, there's the typical sappy "Roses are red, violets are blue, blah blah blah" poetry. There's a type of poetry from Asia called a haiku. There's the sonnet, which was made famous by people such as William Shakespeare. There's even poetry called free verse, which is poetry that doesn't rhyme!

What!? Poems don't all rhyme? What kind of poetry is that? It's still all sappy love stuff, though. Isn't it?

Not at all, Chi. If love poems don't keep your interest, then there are plenty of other types of poems for you to read. However, reading some love poems may not be such a bad idea. Some are romantic. You know, dropping a few lines of vintage poetry may really impress your significant other, more so than cheesy boy-band songs. OK, if you don't want to read love poems, you can read things like the *Iliad* or the *Odyssey,* which are called epic poems. Epic poems are like action movies, but they are in poetry instead of on film, complete with heroes and villains to make it interesting. If action isn't your thing, you might be interested in more philosophical poetry or maybe political poetry. Then there's poetry about flowers and trees and that sort of thing. Still not interested? Try some Edgar Allan Poe; his stuff will creep you out and give you nightmares. Rather have some more abstract stuff? Find some stream of consciousness poetry, and try to figure out what the heck the author, or poet, is trying to say!

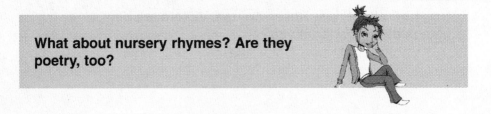

What about nursery rhymes? Are they poetry, too?

Well, Chi, perhaps they are. Is that your favorite poetry? Unfortunately, Chi, we won't be dealing with nursery rhymes here. Maybe you should check out *Get Wise! Mastering Classic Children's Literature*. Just kidding, Chi! Seriously, though, just like we don't have time to get into nursery rhymes, we don't have time to get into each type of poetry.

Excellent! Oops! Did I say that out loud?

Chi, try to be open-minded about this. We're not going to subject you to the "mushy" stuff, but we are going to look at some poetry and practice finding the theme of the poetry. We guarantee that somebody somewhere will make you find the theme of a poem. Hopefully, though, it won't be the person for whom you wrote a poem. Finding the theme of a poem will not be that hard for you. You just have to get into the same frame of mind as the author. With poetry, poets don't just come right out and say what they mean. That wouldn't be poetic, would it? Let's take a look at a classic poem and see what some poetry looks and sounds like:

How do I love thee? Let me count the ways.
I love thee to the depth and breadth and height
My soul can reach, when feeling out of sight
For the ends of Being and ideal Grace.
I love thee to the level of everyday's
Most quiet need, by sun and candle-light.
I love thee freely, as men strive for Right;
I love thee purely, as they turn from Praise.
I love thee with a passion put to use
In my old griefs, and with my childhood's faith.
I love thee with a love I seemed to lose
With my lost saints,—I love thee with the breath,
Smiles, tears, of all my life! —and, if God choose,
I shall but love thee better after death.

Aaahh!! You said no mushy stuff!

Sorry, Chi, but this is a great poem by Elizabeth Barrett Browning, and it *is* perfect for making a few points about poetry. First, did you notice as you read the poem that the end of a line didn't necessarily mean the end of a thought? Poets are just too darn artsy to write a normal thought using a normal sentence. Therefore, thoughts often scroll from one line to the next. Unconventional, sure, but poets are artists, and you know how artists can be! Second, you probably noticed that Browning didn't just come right out and say, "Yo, baby! Let me tell you all the ways I love you: I love you with my soul, I love you day and night, and so on." Again, it just wouldn't be poetic to say it that way. Sweet, maybe, but not poetic! When you read poetry, you just can't skim over it and fly through it. If you do, you'll miss tons of stuff. Take your reading speed down a notch. Read each line carefully, and don't stop your thoughts at the end of each line. Stop your thoughts at punctuation marks. These little tidbits will make reading poetry much easier for you. Now, let's try to find the theme of the poem. Go back, and read it again using the tips we just gave you.

Aw, man! I have to read that again? Well, all right.

You probably realized that the topic or subject of the poem is love. So what is the theme? In other words, what did the author say about love? She listed the ways she loved her loved one, her husband. So the theme of this poem is a wife's love for her husband. That wasn't so complicated, was it? Let's look at one more passage before we try one in a chapter review. You better bundle up for this one.

And now the STORM-BLAST came, and he
Was tyrannous and strong:
He struck with his o'ertaking wings,
And chased south along.

With sloping masts and dipping prow,
As who pursued with yell and blow
Still treads the shadow of his foe
And forward bends his head,
The ship drove fast, loud roared the blast,
And southward aye we fled.

And now there came both mist and snow,
And it grew wondrous cold:
And ice, mast-high, came floating by,
As green as emerald.

And through the drifts the snowy clifts
Did send a dismal sheen:
Nor shapes of men nor beasts we ken—
The ice was all between.

The ice was here, the ice was there,
The ice was all around:
It cracked and growled, and roared and howled,
Like noises in a swound!

Which of the following is the theme of the previous passage?

(A) The frozen, open sea is frightening.

(B) Ice

(C) Cold water and cold weather

(D) A ship in trouble

This is an excerpt from a cool and famous poem by Samuel Taylor Coleridge called *Rime of the Ancient Mariner*. You probably figured out that the passage is about a ship and ice and a storm. But remember, the theme is what the author says about the topic or subject. Wouldn't you agree that he describes the sea and the ice and the storm as scary? If so, you probably overcame your brain-freeze and chose choice **(A)**. See, reading poetry and finding the theme isn't that hard.

You just have to use your brain a little more than you would if you were reading a newspaper or a magazine.

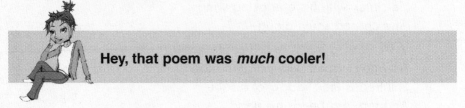

Hey, that poem was *much* cooler!

Before we do the review, let's review what we learned about poetry.

- ★ We learned that Chi doesn't like sappy love poems.
- ★ There are many kinds of poems besides sappy love poems.
- ★ To read these poems, you have to slow down and pay attention to every word and every line.
- ★ To comprehend a poem, try to read the complete thoughts in it instead of reading one line at a time; lines of poetry rarely contain a complete thought.
- ★ Try to imagine the big picture in your mind.

Get Wise!

Read the following poem and answer the question that follows.

Gaily bedight,
A gallant knight,
In sunshine and in shadow,
Had journeyed long,
Singing a song,
In search of Eldorado.
But he grew old-
This knight so bold-
And o'er his heart a shadow
Fell as he found
No spot of ground
That looked like Eldorado.

Which of the following is the theme of the previous poem, an excerpt from Edgar Allan Poe's *Eldorado*?

(A) A knight on a quest

(B) Eldorado

(C) A knight

(D) Eldorado doesn't exist.

How Wise?

(D) Eldorado doesn't exist.

chapter 24

It All Depends on Your Point of View

OK, you've been doing a lot of reading, so it's time to do some physical activity, some exercise. Here's what you need to do. Look around the room, and find an object. It doesn't matter what it is. Look around, and find something. It can be anything from your TV to a pile of dirty clothes to your bratty little brother to the grilled-cheese sandwich you left on your bookshelf last week. Now, put the book down for minute and look at the object closely. OK, now lie down on the floor and look at the same object for another minute. Go ahead, get down there, and stare. OK, now sit up on a chair. Let's go, get up there! When you get up there, look at that same object one last time.

OK, now that I've had my exercise for the week ... what was the point of that!?

Thanks for being a good sport, Chi. There is a method to our madness. You looked at the same object from three different angles, three different perspectives, or three different points of view. You saw the same nasty grilled-cheese sandwich from different points of view, but it's still the same leftover sandwich. Believe it or not, writers use point of view when they write, and you need to know the difference between the different points of view. Just like in your little exercise, writers have three points of view from which they can write. Each one is a little different from the others. First, writers can write in first person. First-person passages are written from the writer's point of view, and the author uses words such as *I*, *me*, *we,* and *us*. When authors write in first person, the reader gets a chance to see inside the author's mind. The reader sees what the author sees, hears what the author hears, or smells what the author smells. First-person passages can be great for figuring out exactly what's going on in an author's brain.

I don't know if I really want to know what an author sees, hears, and especially smells!

The second point of view is called, strangely enough, second person. Second-person passages speak directly to you, the reader. *You* should do this, and *you* might try that. Passages in second person might give instructions or might offer advice. The only way you'll find out what's in the author's brain is if the author speaks directly to you and tells you what is going on in his or her cranium.

Hey, this book is second person!

You got it, Chi! Now, the first two viewpoints are easy to remember, because the first point of view is called first person and the second point of view is called second person. However, the third point of view may be tough to remember, because for some strange reason, it's called third person. Who came up with the names for those points of view? Anyway, third person is the most objective point of view from which an author can write. When you read a third-person reading passage, you are an objective observer who watches as the action unfolds or as the scene develops. Key words to help you identify third-person passages are *he*, *she*, *they*, *those*, *his*, and the like. In addition, third-person passages may use proper nouns for the subjects of sentences instead of pronouns. If you don't know what those are, pick up a copy of *Get Wise! Mastering Grammar Skills* (yet another shameless plug!). In a third-person passage, you only see the picture that the author paints for you. If the author wants you to know something, then you will read about it, but you will not have special insight into what the author is thinking. Also, you will not have special suggestions, advice, or other such information directed especially at you. Imagine you are on the outside of a house looking in at something going on in the living room. That's third person.

Hey, I don't want to be a peeping Chi!

Don't worry, Chi. You'll only see what the author wants you to see. Let's look at some sentences that have been surgically extracted from other reading passages. In the blank space next to each sentence, write 1 if the sentence is written in the first-person point of view, write 2 if the sentence is written in the second-person point of view, and write, you guessed it, 3 if the sentence is written in the third-person point of view. After you label the sentences, check your answers against the correct answers that follow.

____ **1.** He ran so fast that he actually came out of his shoes.

____ **2.** You would be crazy to eat the Atomic Fire and Brimstone Hot Wings from the new wings place downtown.

____ **3.** I got up early, got dressed, ate breakfast, and walked all the way down to the bus stop in the rain before I realized it was Saturday.

____ **4.** Clara's mom was so freaked by Clara's fake tattoo that she fainted onto the kitchen floor.

____ **5.** When you go camping, you should always shake out your shoes before you put them on in the morning so you don't stick your foot in on top of a spider or scorpion.

____ **6.** We were so loud in the movie theater that the old couple in front of us turned around and dumped soda and popcorn on us.

____ **7.** She sneezed so hard that she blew a hole in the tissue.

____ **8.** They ran over to them and said that he wanted to see her again tomorrow.

____ **9.** You may want to start saving your money now if you want to buy front-row tickets for the big concert next summer.

____ **10.** Valentine's Day made her sad, because her boyfriend always buys her chocolates and she's allergic to chocolate.

Let's see how you did. Numbers 3 and 6 are first person. Numbers 2, 5, and 9 are second person. Numbers 1, 4, 7, 8, and 10 are third person. That was pretty easy, wasn't it? So what difference does point of view make in a reading passage? Point of view can completely change the complexion of a reading passage. Let's take a look at the same reading passage written from the three different points of view.

> Imagine for a moment a beautiful day, a great day for a walk. I walk down a path into the woods. I walk along without a care in the world, when all of a sudden a skunk walks onto the path just ahead of me. I stop dead in my tracks. The skunk looks at me, and I look at him. The skunk

stares me down and then lifts his tail. Before I manage to take a single step backward, I smell rotten, wretched, and just plain rank. When I get home, I take three showers and I even bathe in lemon juice. Nothing helps. Now, people run from me when I walk down the street, and babies cry as I pass them because I stink so badly.

Imagine for a moment a beautiful day, a great day for a walk. You walk down a path into the woods. You walk along without a care in the world, when all of a sudden a skunk walks onto the path just ahead of you. You stop dead in your tracks. The skunk looks at you, and you look at him. The skunk stares you down and then lifts his tail. Before you manage to take a single step backward, you smell rotten, wretched, and just plain rank. When you get home, you take three showers and you even bathe in lemon juice. Nothing helps. Now, people run from you when you walk down the street, and babies cry as you pass them because you stink so badly.

Imagine for a moment a beautiful day, a great day for a walk. Felix walks down a path into the woods. He walks along without a care in the world, when all of a sudden a skunk walks onto the path just ahead of him. Felix stops dead in his tracks. The skunk looks at Felix, and Felix looks at him. The skunk stares him down and then lifts his tail. Before Felix manages to take a single step backward, he smells rotten, wretched, and just plain rank. When he gets home, he takes three showers and he even bathes in lemon juice. Nothing helps. Now, people run from Felix when he walks down the street, and babies cry as he passes them because he stinks so badly.

Man, that story stinks!

There you have it. Same story from three perspectives. The first passage was written in first person, the second story was written in second person, and the third story was written in, you guessed it, third person. But you already knew that, didn't you? Let's review this chapter briefly before we do a review exercise. Authors use point of view to affect reading passages. If an author wants to give insight into his or her mind or thoughts, he or she can write in first person, using such words as *I* and *me*. If an author wants to speak directly to you, the reader, just as we are doing now, he or she can write in second person. Obviously, if an author writes to you, then he or she will use words such as *you* in second-person writing. Now remember, this is where it gets complicated. The *third* point-of-view form is called *third* person. Should we repeat that one for you? Third person is the most objective point of view, and it uses words such as *he*, *her,* or even proper nouns. An author can vary the point of view of a story depending on what he or she wants you to know and depending on how he or she wants to speak to you.

I think I want to try to become the first person to write in fourth person!

Good, Chi. You keep working on that. Before you get too wrapped up in that, though, try this review to make sure you've mastered this skill.

Get Wise!

Read the following passages and answer the questions that follow.

Passage A—I was in such a hurry that I totally forgot to grab my raincoat and umbrella before I left. I got to work before it started raining, but the bottom fell out before I got out of my car. I had to run across two parking lots in the pouring rain. I was drenched, and my presentation was soaked and ruined. My new leather shoes got water spots all over them. I was miserable. Then, to make matters worse, my wet hair dripped water into my keyboard and shorted out my computer. This knocked out the network, and nobody got any work done until after lunch. I sure wish I hadn't forgotten my raincoat and umbrella.

Passage B—Jose Smith was so excited to attend his first Major League Baseball game, and he was even more excited to be attending a baseball game on opening day. He had always wanted to see a professional baseball game in person. He was so nervous as he anticipated the first pitch. He felt much better, though, when everyone in the stadium stood on their feet and sang, "Jose, can you see?" He figured that his dad must have set that up.

Passage C—You really should consider watching the game at home this weekend. You may have to pay as much as $100 for the tickets. Then, you will have to pay between $5 and $10 just to park. If you get hungry, you better plan on spending $4 for a soda, $8 for a hamburger, $4 for a hot dog, $3 for a bottled water, and $4 for peanuts. If you eat all that, you can count on spending another $5 for antacid pills to tackle your heartburn. Then, at the end of the game, you'll have to battle 50,000 other fans to get out of the stadium, out of the parking lot, and onto the freeway. Take my advice, and just stay home.

1. Which of the previous passages is written in first person?

   (A) A

   (B) B

   (C) C

2. Which of the previous passages is the most objective of the three passages?

   (A) A

   (B) B

   (C) C

3. In which of the previous passages does the author attempt to connect personally with the reader?

   (A) A

   (B) B

   (C) C

How Wise?

1. **(A)** Passage A
2. **(B)** Passage B
3. **(C)** Passage C

chapter 25

Similes, Metaphors, and Personification, Oh My!

Remember a few chapters ago when we said that authors often think of themselves as artists, so they try to make their work as artsy as possible? Remember when we said that authors sometimes choose not to just say what they mean but rather choose some fancy way of expressing their ideas? Well, that's the focus of this chapter. If you can't recognize symbolism, metaphors, and examples of personification, you are going to make some pretty silly assumptions and perhaps some embarrassing mistakes. Let's face it, you don't want to be like the cheerleader who read about "the industrial giant located in Detroit" and thought that a giant robot had attacked the city. You don't want to be like the big offensive lineman who read about "stormy conditions inside Congress" and thought the Congress had a hole in the roof that was letting in rain.

Sounds like those guys are symbols of dimwittedness!

You got that right, Chi. You may remember from English class that authors use things like similes and metaphors to make their writing more interesting and creative. A simile is a comparison between two seemingly unlike objects using the words *like* or *as*. For example, "that dog is as dumb as a brick" is a good example of a simile. Likewise, "that dog is a dodo" is a good example of a metaphor. A metaphor is a comparison between two seemingly unlike objects without the use of *like* or *as*. Authors use both of these techniques all the time, but they use the metaphor more often on a large scale, so we'll look at that tool first. In other words, an author can use a metaphor throughout a story to make his or her point, or the author can use an entire story as a metaphor.

Let me try one. This book is a compass in a confusing world of reading passages.

Hey, not bad, Chi! You have the idea. To find the metaphor in a reading passage or to figure out to what the reading passage refers, metaphorically, you have to use some of those same skills we've been practicing for many chapters now. You have to recognize the main idea of the passage and see the big picture. You have to also read between the lines to figure out exactly what the author is trying to say. This is old hat for you by now. You just have to put these skills to use in a new way. Let's look at a reading passage in which the author uses the metaphor to make the reading passage more interesting. Read the passage, and then answer the questions that follow.

The young artist carefully surveyed his canvas and mapped out his plan in his mind. With brilliant brush strokes, the artist went to work on his masterpiece, a life-sized mural of abstract art. First red, then blue, and then yellow, green, and purple. The artist, with touch of a young master, carefully yet whimsically blended and mixed the colors until the entire surface of the canvas was covered. The artist stood for a moment and admired his work. He decided, however, to add more colors, more texture, and more feeling to his masterpiece. After a few final strokes of genius, the artist stood back and viewed his mural with great satisfaction. Then, suddenly, acting in a moment of inspiration, the artist decided to extend the mural onto a human canvas. The artist covered his body inch by inch with all the colors of the rainbow until he was a walking masterpiece. Just as the artist finished the greatest creation of his young career, he was discovered. The woman stood and stared in disbelief at the art she found.

1. The "young artist" is a metaphor for which of the following?

(A) A teenage artist

(B) An artist with little art experience

(C) An old artist

(D) A young child

2. The previous reading passage is a metaphor for which of the following?

(A) A young, talented artist being discovered by an agent

(B) A young, talented artist being discovered by an art critic

(C) A young child being caught making a mess by his mother

(D) A child being discovered by a talent agent

In this passage, the author describes a young child, maybe even a toddler, who was painting all over a wall and then on himself. Then, after the "masterpiece" is finished, the child's mother walks in to find the "art" all over everything. Can't you just picture this? Heck, you may even remember this! The author uses the "young artist" as a metaphor for the young child, and the entire passage is a metaphor for the scene we just described. Therefore, as you probably figured out, the answers for the questions are **(D)** a young child and **(C)** a young child being caught making a mess by his mother. Do you see how the author used these metaphors as symbolism?

I remember an incident similar to that one that happened a long time ago ...

A literary tool that is similar to a metaphor is a *simile*. A simile, as we said earlier, is a comparison between to seemingly unlike things. The catch is that a simile uses the words *like* or *as*. For example, "the teacher is as mean as a hornet" and "the teacher growled like a bear" are two textbook examples of similes. In most normal circumstances, teachers and hornets have little or nothing in common. Same goes for teachers and bears. But with a well-thought-out simile, a teacher can be like a hornet, a bear, an ogre, a villain, or pretty much anything the author wants. Pretty clever, huh?

Now let's take a look at *personification*, another kind of symbolism that authors use to make their writing more interesting. Personification is a tool authors use to make a nonhuman object have humanlike qualities. An author can do this by giving human characteristics or traits to something that isn't human. For example, "the locker bit my hand" and "the algebra test stared back at me" are two good examples of personification. Lockers don't have teeth, and tests don't have eyes, right? Of course not. But anything goes in literature! In some cases, an author could use an entire paragraph of personification to describe something. In a case like that, you need to use the same skills you used with the metaphors to determine what the author is describing or what the author is trying to say. Let's take a good look at such a passage.

The trees reached out and grabbed at Little Red Riding Hood as she ran through the forest. The moon stared down on her as she ran. The wind ran its fingers through her hair and tried to spook her as she went on her way to Grandma's house. As she ran and ran, the wolf howled at the moon. Little Red Riding Hood ran like a deer all the way home.

1. Which of the following is *not* an example of personification?
   (A) Trees reached out and grabbed
   (B) Wind ran its fingers through her hair
   (C) Wolf howled
   (D) Little Red Riding Hood ran like a deer
2. Which of the following is a simile?
   (A) Trees reached out and grabbed
   (B) Wind ran its fingers through her hair
   (C) Wolf howled
   (D) Little Red Riding Hood ran like a deer

That was a little creepier than I remember! Yikes!

Maybe it was creepier, but you have to admit it was more interesting reading than the traditional story of Red. The answers, by the way, are **(C)** and **(D)**. Remember that to make the most of this symbolism, you have to see the big picture and figure out what the author is trying to say. Additionally, read between the lines to see what the author is implying. These little tips will help you to avoid the mistakes of the cheerleader and the offensive lineman. We sure don't want you to end up like those two at the beginning of this chapter. Let's do a quick review exercise before we move on to the next chapter. Dive into the review exercise like a diver jumps into a pool.

How about, "That was so corny, you should feed it to the horse you rode in on?"

Get Wise!

For each of the following statements, use "S" to identify a statement as a simile, "M" to identify a statement as a metaphor, and "P" to identify a statement as personification.

_____ **1.** His locker smelled like a garbage dump.

_____ **2.** The shirt swallowed her, but she wore it anyway.

_____ **3.** The mighty warriors battled for nine innings, and, in the end, they emerged victorious.

_____ **4.** Her makeup looked like a box of crayons melted on her face.

_____ **5.** He's as smart as an elephant is fat, but she's about as smart as an elephant is skinny.

_____ **6.** The pizza called my name, and I couldn't resist the temptation.

_____ **7.** The swimming pool looked inviting, but the water was as frigid as the Arctic Ocean.

_____ **8.** We ran as fast as we could, but the bus pulled away and taunted us all the way down the street.

_____ **9.** The statue looked at the class, and every person in the class froze in his or her tracks.

_____ **10.** The carpet in the hallway told strange tales of spilled drinks, dropped gum, tracked-in mud, and who knows what else.

How Wise?

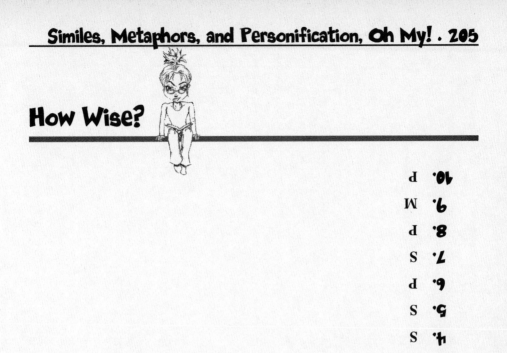

1. S
2. P
3. M
4. S
5. S
6. P
7. S
8. P
9. M
10. P

chapter 26

Mood or 'Tude

"Watch your tone!" How many times have you had a teacher or parent say that to you? If you're a normal teenager anywhere on this planet, this phrase is probably familiar to you. Did you respond with "Sorry, I didn't mean it that way," to let them know that what you said just came out wrong? Sometimes it isn't what you say that gets you in trouble but rather how you say it. You know exactly what we're talking about. The same principle applies to reading and writing. Take the phrase "Gee, thanks a lot," for example. If you read the phrase by itself, do you really know how the author wants it to sound? We'll show you what we mean. Let's say that your mom surprised you with Pearl Jam tickets. Your response would be "Gee, thanks a lot." Now let's say that you're walking through the cafeteria and a kid trips and spills his lunch tray full of chocolate milk, beef stew, mashed potatoes and gravy, and tapioca pudding all over your new outfit. Your response would be "Gee, thanks a lot," but you would obviously mean it in a totally different way. Finally, your grandmother buys you a birthday present. You open the present, and it's a lime green velour leisure suit and a pair of white patent-leather shoes. Your response would be "Gee, thanks a lot," but you would mean this in a completely different way than the first two times you used it.

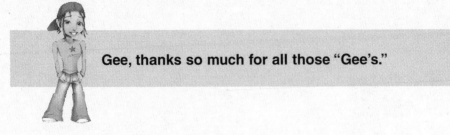

Gee, thanks so much for all those "Gee's."

Watch your tone, Chi. How about one more quick example to further make our point? Let's look at the word "Whatever." If your mom says, "Would you rather have meat loaf or liver and onions for dinner," then you might respond with "Whatever." If your best friend shows up at school and says, "I just saw Ben Affleck and, oh my gosh, he smiled at me," you would respond with "Whatever." The same phrase used two different ways can be effective when speaking, but it can be confusing in writing. When you say phrases such as "Gee, thanks a lot" and "Whatever," you can place emphasis on whatever part of the phrase you want to let the listener know if you are being nice or really sarcastic. Writers don't have that luxury, so they have to pay close attention to the tone of their writing. The tone of a reading passage sets the mood or the attitude of the passage. That's pretty much the same way tone works when you speak. You set the mood or the 'tude of the conversation with your tone. Right, Chi?

Yeah, whatever!

If tone is so important, how do writers set the tone and why does it make any difference to you? The biggest way that an author sets the tone of a reading passage is through word choice. Because a book on tape is about the only way you can figure out exactly how an author wants a passage to sound, the next best thing for you to do is to pay close attention to word choice. Let's see what a big difference word choice can make in the tone of a reading passage.

1. The kids arrived at the car wash more than an hour late and got to work soaping the vehicles.
2. The arrogant kids begrudgingly arrived at the car wash more than an hour late and finally got to work sloppily soaping the vehicles.
3. The embarrassed kids finally arrived at the car wash more than an hour late and quickly got to work diligently soaping the vehicles.

The first sentence is pretty blah and unemotional. Who knows what point the author wants to make, because the author just gives some facts. The second sentence has more of a cynical, sarcastic, and irritated tone. Did you see the key words *arrogant*, *finally,* and *sloppily*? That indicates that the author isn't trying to paint such a pretty picture. In the third sentence, the author uses a more sympathetic tone. Did you see the key words *embarrassed*, *quickly,* and *diligently*? The tone isn't nearly as harsh as in the second sentence.

Let's think back to the last chapter for a minute. Still remember what we learned in the last chapter about similes, metaphors, and personification? Let's hope so! Authors use these tools all the time to set the tone of a passage. Let's look at a few examples of how symbolism can affect the tone of a reading passage.

1. The principal walked through the halls of the school looking for students who were supposed to be in class.
2. The warden stormed the passageways of the prison searching for convicts who were supposed to be in their cells.
3. The zookeeper strolled through the zoo looking for monkeys who were supposed to be in their cages.

Hmm ... do I detect just a hint of sarcasm and cynicism?

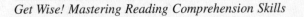

You got it, Chi! The author certainly made the second two sentences more interesting than the first one. With just a few choice words, an author can totally change the tone of a sentence, a paragraph, a chapter, or even an entire book. Test-writers love to ask questions about the tone in which an author has written a particular piece of literature, so it's pretty darn important that you look for tone. Let's try a quick practice passage. Look for key words that indicate the way an author would want the passage to sound.

> The chess team at Garfield High is pathetic. Those geeks don't know the difference between a rook and a rock. Their training regimen consists of nothing more than a few practice games on Novice Level of some old, out-of-date chess software on their calculators. Every time they get together, they spend most of their time gawking at the hot chicks from the checkers club across the hall. In fact, to them, the word "check" means "Hey, hot chick across the hall—check her out!" Truth be told, the chess team is as clueless as the cheerleading squad.

Which of the following best describes the tone of the previous passage?

(A) Lighthearted

(B) Disrespectful

(C) Insincere

(D) Serious

Apparently, that author doesn't think too highly of the chess team. You probably made the right choice and selected choice **(B)**. Finding the tone in a typical reading passage should be a piece of cake for you after all the reading you've done in this book. But what about poetry? Do you think you can find the tone of a poem?

Finding the tone in poetry is pretty much the same as with any other piece of literature. Look for key words and clues that indicate how the author wants the poem to come across. Symbolism is common in poetry, and it will offer some good clues about a poem's tone. Let's look at a few quick examples so you can practice looking for the tone in poetry.

If it's a romantic love poem, I can tell you right now that the tone is sappy!

Ah, distinctly I remember it was in the bleak December,
And each separate dying ember wrought its ghost upon the floor.
Eagerly I wished the morrow;—vainly I had sought to borrow
From my books surcease of sorrow—sorrow for the lost Lenore—
For the rare and radiant maiden whom the angels name Lenore—
Nameless here for evermore.
And the silken sad uncertain rustling of each purple curtain
Thrilled me—filled me with fantastic terrors never felt before;
So that now, to still the beating of my heart, I stood repeating,
"'Tis some visitor entreating entrance at my chamber door—
Some late visitor entreating entrance at my chamber door;—
This it is, and nothing more."

1. Which of the following best describes the tone of the previous passage, an excerpt from Edgar Allan Poe's *The Raven*?

(A) Gloomy

(B) Cheery

(C) Fantastic

(D) Optimistic

Live with me, and be my love,
And we will all the pleasures prove,
That hills and valleys, dales and fields,
And all the craggy mountains yields.

There will we sit upon the rocks,
And see the shepherds feed their flocks,
By shallow rivers, by whose falls
Melodious birds sing madrigals.

There will I make thee a bed of roses,
With a thousand fragrant posies,
A cap of flowers, and a kirtle
Embroider'd all with leaves of myrtle.

A belt of straw and ivy buds,
With coral clasps and amber studs;
And if these pleasures may thee move,
Then live with me and be my love.

2. Which of the following best describes the tone of the previous passage, a sonnet by William Shakespeare?

(A) Delightful

(B) Serious

(C) Repentant

(D) Religious

You should have included "disgustingly romantic and sappy" as one of the answer choices for the second poem!

The two passages were obviously as different as night and day, but you probably had no problem figuring out the tone of the two. In the first poem, the spooky way that Poe wrote gives it a gloomy tone, so the answer obviously is **(A)**. As Chi pointed out, the second poem certainly is romantic, but what was the tone of the romantic poem? Shakespeare tried to make this a happy, optimistic sonnet, so the tone is pretty darn delightful; therefore, the answer is **(A)**.

Let's review this chapter quickly, because we know you're chomping at the bit to get through the rest of this book so you can start the book over again. Tone is basically the mood or attitude of a reading passage. Because many authors of literature have been dead for hundreds of years, they can't be around to tell you exactly how they want their writing to sound. Therefore, they used tools like descriptive language, similes, metaphors, and personification to set the tone. Understanding tone is important, because if you don't understand the tone of a passage, you may miss the point of the passage. Likewise, misunderstanding the tone of one of your best friend's comments may leave you thinking she was being nice when she was being sarcastic to you!

Whatever!

Get Wise

Read the following passages and answer the question that follows each passage.

The new book will be pretty good, I think. The author seemed like he put a lot of hard work into it. Hopefully, the book will have some nice artwork, but we haven't seen it yet. The idea for the book is like a daring fashion trend—the general public may accept it, or it may not. The writing might be pretty good, because I think the author has written a book once before. Maybe the book will sell enough copies to keep the book out of the bargain bins at the bookstore.

1. Which of the following best describes the tone of the previous passage?

(A) Critical

(B) Insecure

(C) Harsh

(D) Inquisitive

The old man shuffled out onto his driveway and down toward his hammock. The breeze blew gently, and the clouds floated softly overhead. The birds in the trees sang lullaby after lullaby as the man settled into the hammock. The trees reached over the hammock and shaded the hammock from the sun. The breeze stroked the man's hair and helped him relax. The hammock swung to and fro like a baby's cradle, and the man drifted into a deep slumber.

2. Which of the following best describes the tone of the previous passage?

(A) Tense

(B) Sarcastic

(C) Peaceful

(D) Complimentary

Selling lemons is his job
Or maybe ones attacked by a mob
Or maybe rides that squeak and rattle
Or rides with seats that smell like cattle.
Convincing you that you need a car
Can make this guy a resale star
Especially if you pay full price
For a hoopty complete with fuzzy dice.

3. Which of the following best describes the tone of the previous passage?

(A) Critical

(B) Inquisitive

(C) Authoritative

(D) Humorous

How Wise?

1. (B) Insecure

2. (C) Peaceful

3. (D) Humorous

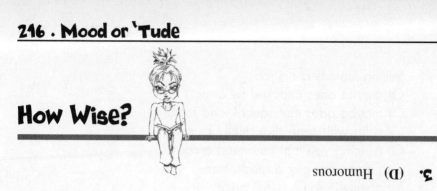

chapter 27

Got Lit?

You've probably done more reading lately than you ever have before. You are going to encounter all sorts of literature as you keep reading in the future. We could write a dozen different books, all of which we're sure you'd buy and read cover to cover, on how to read and comprehend literature, but we've covered the basics here. If you keep the last several chapters of information locked away in your brain, you're well on your way to becoming a literature professor. No, we're just kidding! Seriously, though, you have enough lit-reading info now to handle most any question you'll see about basic literature comprehension. We know that after getting this far into this book, your brain is almost full, so we'll just get right into the review of the lit chapters.

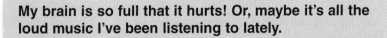

My brain is so full that it hurts! Or, maybe it's all the loud music I've been listening to lately.

One of the most basic skills you need for being successful when dealing with literature, besides choosing the right caffeine-filled beverage, is finding the theme of a piece of literature. Let's see what you learned about the theme in literature.

- ★ The theme is not what the reading passage is about; that's the subject or topic. Rather, the theme is what the author says about the subject or topic.
- ★ To find the theme, look for the implied main idea and read between the lines.
- ★ Try to see the big picture, especially when you're looking for the theme in a long reading passage or even in an entire book.
- ★ Finding the theme of a work of prose or a work of poetry is basically the same. You may have to pay a little closer attention to detail in poetry, but the concept is the same.

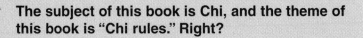

The subject of this book is Chi, and the theme of this book is "Chi rules." Right?

Have you been reading the same book as everyone else, Chi? Maybe you should review Chapter 1. Maybe it's just a matter of perspective, Chi. Speaking of perspective, the next big skill involved in comprehending literature is finding the author's point of view. Here's a quick refresher of point of view.

- ★ Point of view is an author's perspective, the perspective from which the reading passage was written.
- ★ The first point of view is called first person and provides an insight into what the author is thinking. In first-person writing, the author uses words such as *I*, *me*, *we*, *our,* and the like.
- ★ The second point of view is known as second person. This type of writing is directed at you, the reader. The author uses this to speak directly

to the reader. In second-person writing, the author uses the word *you,* maybe even *y'all* if he or she is from the South.

★ The third point of view is called third person. This is the most objective perspective, because it treats the reader as an observer of the action in the text. In third-person writing, the author uses words such as *he*, *she*, *they*, *him*, *her,* and *them*.

I've almost perfected the art of writing in fourth person. Look for my first book to hit the shelves soon!

The next literary skill you learned was how to identify symbolism in literature. You certainly don't want to make the embarrassing mistake of taking something literally when it was only intended to be symbolic. Here are a few quick reminders.

★ Similes are comparisons between two seemingly unlike things using the words *like* or *as*. An example is "the biology teacher is as old as the fossil on her shelf."

★ Metaphors are comparisons between two seemingly unlike things without the use of *like* or *as*. An example is "the biology teacher is a dinosaur."

★ Metaphors can be as simple as a sentence or as elaborate as an entire reading passage.

★ Personification is when an author gives humanlike qualities to a nonhuman object. An example of personification is "the cash machine devoured my cash card and then chuckled a series of beeps and blips."

When it comes to Chi, there are no comparisons!

Watch your tone, Chi! Hey, that was a great setup for a segue, Chi. The last skill we worked on was understanding the tone of a passage. We've all been corrected for our tone before, but that's probably just because we didn't know how to correctly convey the tone we wanted to convey. Right? Let's review what you need to know about tone.

- ★ The tone of a reading passage is basically the mood or the 'tude (attitude for those of you who haven't figured that out yet!) of the reading passage. Authors use tone to help the reader understand exactly how the reading should sound.
- ★ Authors use key words, especially similes, metaphors, and personification, to set the tone of a passage.
- ★ There are as many possible tones of literature, both poetry and prose, as there are moods that an author might want to convey. A reading passage's tone could be serious, humorous, creepy, uplifting, serious, and so on.

There you have it: the nuts and bolts of reading and understanding literature. If you can keep these simple things in mind as you're reading literature, you'll be well on your way to good comprehension of the literature. We've practiced each of these individually, but let's see how you do when you have to be on the lookout for all these things at once. Take a deep breath, grab a quick snack, and jump right into the review.

We're so close to the end of this book that I can smell it! And it smells good!

Get Wise!

Read the following passages, and answer the questions that follow each passage. Remember to read each passage carefully, and pay attention to things like theme, symbolism, and tone.

> Patrick constantly sought the attention of the other kids in his class. One day in the cafeteria, the class clown challenged Patrick to a stew contest. Patrick gladly accepted the challenge. The class clown, Lester, went through the lunch line and selected several offerings from the hot-lunch counter. Patrick did the same. Once the two warriors were seated at their table, each stirred the contents of his meal tray into a single large bowl. Each of the two was determined to win the contest, so each selected things like spinach, vanilla pudding, gravy, chocolate milk, meat loaf, beets, carrots, and bread pudding for their stews. When they finished stirring their concoctions, they exchanged bowls. The goal of the contest was to be the first to eat the entire bowl of "stew" prepared by the other contestant. The students in the cafeteria picked sides and stood behind their warrior to cheer on his effort. The warriors stared deeply into one another's eyes and then chowed down on their chow. Lester got off to a quick start and so did Patrick. Then, Lester hit a particularly lumpy bite of stew that nearly made him gag. That brief pause gave Patrick just enough time to gulp down the remaining bites of stew. As he slurped the last of the stew from the bowl, the students behind him erupted with cheers and applause. Patrick had toppled the king of comedy and had claimed the title of class clown.

1. Which of the following did the author use to write the previous passage?

(A) First-person point of view

(B) Second-person point of view

(C) Third-person point of view

(D) Chi's nearly perfected fourth-person point of view

2. Which of the following was used as a metaphor in the previous passage?

(A) Clown

(B) Warriors

(C) Stew

(D) Students

3. Which of the following best describes the tone of the previous passage?

(A) Gloomy

(B) Passionate

(C) Suspenseful

(D) Indifferent

Today's generation of moviegoers, in my opinion, detract from the whole movie experience. Today's whippersnappers annoy me more and more every time I go to the movies now. I hear cell phones ringing with crazy ring tones. I hear beepers or pagers or whatever those crazy kids call them these days. Kids get up and walk around during the movie. We never did that when we were kids. Kids throw popcorn and slurp their drinks. When we were that age, we worked for weeks at a time just to get the extra money for popcorn. We sure didn't throw it around the theater. The thing that drives me most crazy, though, is when those kids pair up and neck in the middle of the movie. We never even did that sort of thing back in the day. Some of the kids nowadays wear the craziest clothes I've ever seen when they go to the movies. Some of the outfits look like costumes from a vaudeville show. We used to dress up in our best clothes for a trip to the movies. And then there's the talking. The kids talk to each other like long-lost friends who haven't seen each other in years. When we were kids, we didn't talk because we paid a whole nickel to get in and we weren't going to waste that kind of money! Maybe I should look into one of those VCR machines that's all the rage these days.

4. Which of the following best describes the tone of the previous passage?

(A) Critical

(B) Hilarious

(C) Romantic

(D) Optimistic

5. Which of the following is the theme of the previous passage?

(A) Movies

(B) Kids at the movies

(C) Today's movie-going kids lack manners.

(D) Old-fashioned movies required more attentiveness.

6. Which of the following did the author use to write the previous passage?

(A) First-person point of view

(B) Second-person point of view

(C) Third-person point of view

(D) Chi's nearly perfected fourth-person point of view

7. Which two of the following are *not* similes?

(A) The craziest clothes

(B) Like costumes from a vaudeville show

(C) Like long-lost friends

(D) Whippersnappers

How Wise?

1. (C) Third-person point of view

2. (B) Warriors

3. (D) Indifferent

4. (A) Critical

5. (C) Today's movie-going kids lack manners.

6. (A) First-person point of view

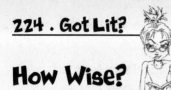

7. (A) **and** (D) The craziest clothes and whippersnappers

I Feel the Need, the Need for ...

Speed! That's what this chapter is about. Speed reading, that is. Have you ever stayed up really late and seen those infomercials that promise you unbelievable speed-reading success in just a few easy lessons? Some of those crazy programs promise that you can read, like, 25,000 words a minute just by taking a special speed-reading course. There's another infomercial that promises that you will learn how to read and memorize an entire textbook in 15 minutes just by fanning through the pages a few times. Oh, did you catch the fine print that promised that you can achieve this amazing success for just three easy payments of $29.95? Ah, then there's the hypnotist who can hypnotize you, for a small fee, of course, and make you capable of reading a page per second just by glancing at the book. Ever seen that guy? How about the old lady who tries to sell wide-angle reading glasses to improve your reading speed? She's a real winner, too.

I wish I could read faster, but I can't afford all those gimmicks on TV!

Then you're in luck, Chi! We're going to offer you some pretty good pointers on how to improve your reading speed at no extra cost to you! That's right! Just because we care, we're throwing in a whole chapter on ways to improve your reading speed. Before we get into some speed-reading strategies that work, let's be clear on a few things. First, there is nothing that will make you read thousands and thousands of words per minute, no matter what the price! That's just garbage! Everyone can stand to improve his or her reading speed a little, but a reading speed of several thousand words per minute isn't realistic. Second, the greatest reading speed in the world won't do you a bit of good if you can't comprehend or remember what you read. Comprehension is more important than speed when it comes to reading. After all, that's why you just read a whole book on reading better, and this is the first chapter you've seen in the book about reading faster! Third, you can't finish this chapter and then expect to read at a lightning-fast pace. Speed reading takes practice—lots of it! You can't read a book about running faster and then go fly like the wind, and the same principle applies here.

I couldn't fly like the wind no matter what I did!

Before we tell you some things to do to read faster, we're going to tell you a few things not to do. First, stop sound-ing out syl-la-bles as you work through read-ing pas-sa-ges be-cause that tech-nique re-du-ces your read-ing speed and com-pre-hen-sion. See what we mean? If you can avoid sounding out every syllable of every word that you read, you'll increase your reading speed and your overall comprehension. Second, if you're the person who sits in the library and reads out loud and drives everybody nuts, then we have one word for you: SHHH!!!!!! You can't read nearly as fast when you read out loud as you can when you read silently. Besides, think about all the people who will no longer throw things at you for reading out loud! Finally, avoid re-reading everything you read. Finally, avoid re-reading everything you read. See how much slower you will move through the reading passage if you have to re-read? See how much slower you will move through the reading passage if you have to re-read? Do you get the point yet? If you re-read an entire paragraph, then you reduce your reading speed by half! If you can avoid those three things, then you will automatically increase your speed, and we haven't even gotten to the good stuff yet!

You know, I could have finished this book a lot sooner if this chapter were at the beginning instead of at the end!

Sorry, Chi. Look at it this way. Now you can start over and read this book faster than you did the first time! Let's get right to the tips. The first tips are things you need to do before you start reading. Start by eliminating as many distractions as you can. You better believe that an episode of *Baywatch* or *The Bachelor* will tempt you to look away from your reading every once in a while. To read faster, you must keep your eyes on the book and not on the hotties! Next, find a place to read where you can read for an extended period of time without having to get up or move or shift or adjust your seat. If you're squirming because you're uncomfortable, then you can't keep your eyes moving through the text. Next, keep your hands on the book. This sounds silly, but you can read faster with your hands on the book. You need to have your hands on the book to turn the pages and keep your rhythm going. If you're using one hand to blow your nose and the other hand to twirl your hair, then you'll have to reach down and fumble with the book to turn the page every few seconds. That will slow you down!

OK, so I should blow my nose before I start reading? Got it!

Finally, decide before you start reading what information you're going to need to get out of your reading. Remember way back at the beginning of the book when we discussed the different reading speeds for different kinds of texts? That comes into play here big time! Just because you are going to increase your reading speed doesn't mean that from this point on you will read everything at the same speed. You will still need to read textbooks at a slower pace than you read the newspaper. Now, though, you can read each kind of reading passage a little faster!

Now, let's get down to the nitty-gritty. Maybe the most important thing you can do is to learn to read groups of words instead of single words. In other words, you are going to read much more quickly if you are seeing three words at a time instead of one word at a time. After all, reading is about concepts and not about individual words. Believe it or not, your eyes can look at several things at one time and your brain can sort it out just as fast as you can move your eyes. Try this. Choose an object somewhere in the room you're in right now that you can look at. When you look at the object, look straight ahead at it, but take notice of the things you can still see in your peripheral vision, or off to the sides. Ready? Try it now. Did you see how wide your field of vision can be? Pretty cool, huh?

Wanna see something really cool? Do it again with your eyes crossed!

Let's do a quick exercise to help you get used to doing the same thing you did in the previous exercise. This time, though, we're going to practice with some word groups. In this exercise, look at the word in the middle column, but see the word in the left column and in the right column at the same time. In other words, look in the middle column and read the three words together. Here's an example:

slimy	**green**	monsters

Did you read "slimy green monsters" when you looked at the middle word? Good. See how this works? Do the following exercise and try to move through the list quickly.

very	**sloppy**	dresser
dogs	**love**	leftovers
men	**don't**	dance
pigs	**smell**	truffles
teachers	**have**	pets
television	**warps**	minds
gymnasts	**play**	checkers
baseball	**players**	rock
pictures	**tell**	stories
toothbrushes	**scrub**	teeth

How did you do? Were you starting to get the hang of it toward the end of the list? Good. Let's do one more list, and we'll move on to the next tip.

crickets	**play**	music
computers	**save**	money
teachers	**eat**	students
words	**are**	random
pizza	**tastes**	yummy
oatmeal	**feels**	bizarre
artists	**paint**	pictures
goldfish	**make**	friends
librarians	**are**	loud
hats	**cover**	bald spots

Great exercise, but I read lines, not columns!

Good point, Chi. Let's take the skill you just practiced and put it to work in a more realistic setting. Try reading the following passage the same way you read the columns above, three or four words at a time.

> My grandmother always told my friends that if we made funny faces, our faces might stay that way. We tried hard to keep our faces stretched and distorted to see if she was right or wrong. Apparently she fibbed or she didn't really know what she was talking about. My friends' faces are really funny but they started out that way when they were born.

Hey, that is a great trick!

Very funny, Chi! It takes practice, but that's a great strategy to help you start reading concepts instead of just words. Just think how much faster you will read when you get really good at seeing several words at once and not just one word at a time. The next important technique is also a visual technique. In other words, you'll need to train your eyes for this, too. One of the biggest stumbling blocks for readers is skipping lines or re-reading the same line or losing track of which line was just completed. Does this sound familiar? Doesn't that just make you nuts when you get to the end of a line and you lose your place on the page? There are two ways to fix this problem. First, you can move your hand or finger along under the lines so you don't lose your place. Some speed-reading experts say that this technique will slow you down, but it is certainly better than the alternative. The second way to overcome this bad habit is to practice. That's right! Just like shooting free throws, playing the piano, square dancing, or whatever, the only way to get better is with practice. Now, truth be told, some books contribute to this problem by printing with tiny print and lines that are stacked one on top of the other. This makes it a little tougher to not get lost. Those kinds of books are the ones you need to practice with, though, if you're going to improve your speed. You just have to train your eyes.

The last speed-reading tip we have to offer is a last resort of sorts. You won't want to use this strategy with everything you read. However, let's say that you have 100 pages of a novel that you have to read for class the next day. You're in big trouble, right? Not necessarily. Especially with novels, selective reading can be pretty effective. As you read through the text, read the first and last sentence of each paragraph. The main idea of a paragraph is often found at the beginning, and, frequently, the sentence that wraps up the paragraph is at the end. If you use this technique, you will have the main idea, and you will see the big picture.

Hey, I just found a new favorite way to read!

Not so fast, Chi! Remember that this isn't necessarily the best way to read, especially if you have to get some good hard facts out of the text. By reading the first and last sentence of each paragraph, you obviously will miss some important information. For example, you may pick up on the idea that the main character of a story is a man from Ireland. You may miss the fact that he has red hair, bad teeth, walks everywhere he goes, and claims to have a leprechaun as a pet.

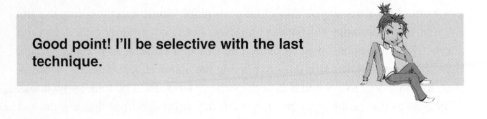

Good point! I'll be selective with the last technique.

Before we bring this chapter to a screeching halt, there are a few other things that are certainly worth mentioning. For starters, if you read slowly because you have to hold the page an inch away from your face, the problem may not be with your technique. The problem may be with your eyes. Second, if you're having trouble figuring out what words mean, then the problem may not be with your technique. The problem may be with your vocabulary. The better your vocabulary is, the faster you'll read. Makes sense, doesn't it? The last tip we're going to give you is practice, practice, practice. Did we mention practice yet? The more you read, the better you'll read. The more you read and practice the strategies we've given you, the faster you'll read. No gimmicks and no magic—just good sound advice and lots of practice. That's all you need, all you need for speed!

Hey, that beats the heck out of babysitting those twins to pay for that speed-reading course! Thanks!

Puzzle 4

Complete the following puzzle using the words you just learned in Chapters 23–28. Puzzle solutions are in the back of the book.

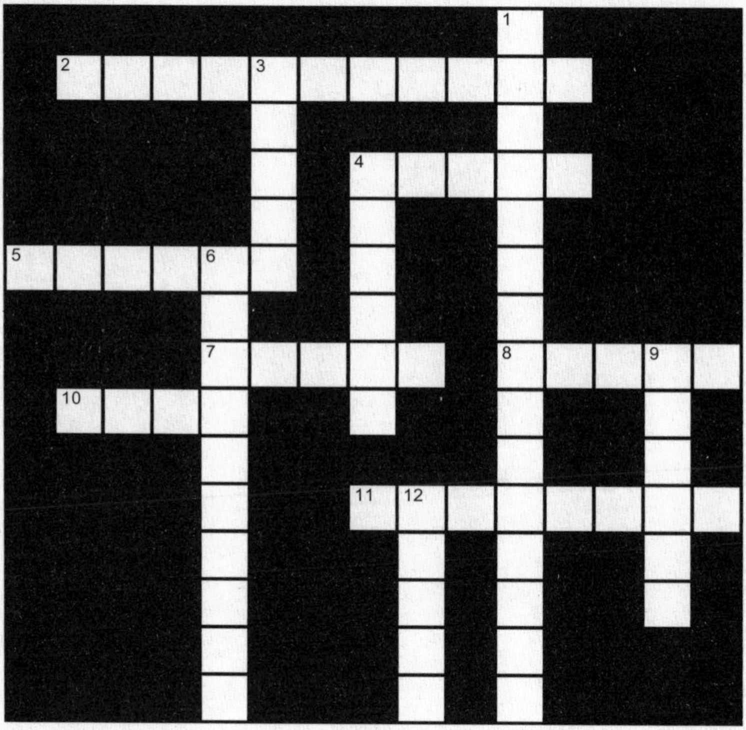

Across

2. PERSPECTIVE FROM WHICH LITERATURE IS WRITTEN

4. LITERATURE THAT ISN'T POETRY

5. COMPARISON USING *LIKE* OR *AS*

7. POINT OF VIEW WRITTEN AS *HE*, *SHE*, *THEY*

8. POINT OF VIEW WRITTEN AS *I*, *ME*, *MY*, *WE*

10. SETS THE MOOD OR ATTITUDE OF LITERATURE

11. COMPARISON OF TWO SEEMINGLY UNLIKE THINGS

Down

1. GIVING HUMAN QUALITIES TO A NON-HUMAN OBJECT

3. WHAT IS SAID ABOUT THE SUBJECT IN LITERATURE

4. HAIKU, SONNETS, FREE VERSE, AND SAPPY STUFF ABOUT LOVE

6. NOVELS, SHORT STORIES, PLAYS, POEMS, AND SO ON

9. POINT OF VIEW WRITTEN AS *YOU*, *YOU*, OR *YOU*

12. POEMS ABOUT A HERO'S ADVENTURE

chapter 29

That's a Wrap, Part 2

It's probably not a secret anymore that the end of the book is just right around the corner. We've been trying to control our emotions, but to be honest, we're really broken up about having to say good-bye. Because we aren't ready to turn you loose yet, however, let's take a little stroll down memory lane.

Gee, can you get a grip, already?

Ok, Chi, we're going to see just how well you've been paying attention during our time together. That's right! We're going to pick your brain a little just to see how many facts stuck. Is it a test? Not exactly. Is it for a grade? No, not really. First of all, you've come this far and there's no point in coming so close to the end of something without seeing it through. Second, one of the biggest challenges for readers is finishing a book. Everybody, at some time or another, wrestles with the dilemma of finishing the book or putting it down.

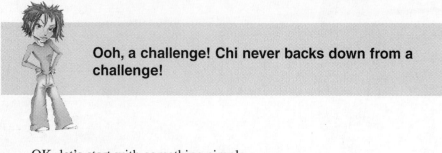

Ooh, a challenge! Chi never backs down from a challenge!

OK, let's start with something simple.

1. At the beginning of the book, we suggested that you put together a survival kit of sorts for reading, basically some tools that you will need to help you out along the way. Remember? OK, list four of those things in the blanks provided below.

2. Here's another easy one. Do you remember three techniques you can use, some of which require the things in the previous blanks, to help you to locate and identify facts in a reading passage?

Write them in the blanks below.

Wow! I can't believe I remember all this!

3. Now, let's see how well you remember some stuff from our award-winning reading passages. According to Luigi Scallopini, what is the most important ingredient or element in a sandwich?

Write your answer here:

(Sorry, Chi, if we're making you hungry again.)

4. Because we're talking about food, let's think back to the reading passage about the ideal breakfast food for today's busy teens. According to the passage, what was the one thing that all the best cereals had in common?

If you remember, write the answer here:

5. Ok, let's really get your mouth watering, Chi. What was it that our old pal Barney sold in record amounts?

If you can recall that, write it here:

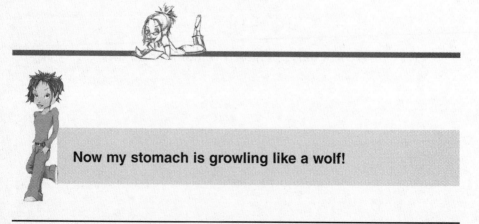

Now my stomach is growling like a wolf!

6. Hey, nice simile, Chi! Let's see what else you remember. How about those crazy old twins? How old were those geezers?

See if you can fit their age in this space:

7. Now, dig deep and see if you can recall the chapter with all the crazy detective references? Anyway, do you remember whose publications the Walker-Hammond detective agency used as training manuals and instructional materials? (Hint—Chi is apparently a big fan!)

Write that answer here:

8. How about this one? Write the name of the world's most boring card game here:

9. Speaking of games, do you remember the game played with dice?

If so, write the answer here:

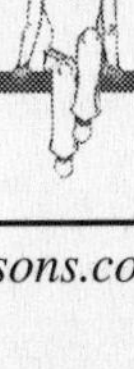

Yeah, I've played both of those games about, hmm ..., *zero* times!

10. Surely some of the highlights of the book were the great chapter titles. Remember the chapter called "Gaze into Your Crystal Ball"? What was the topic of that chapter? (Chi, you probably already knew we were going to ask that question.)

Write the answer here:

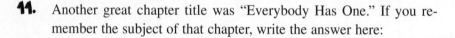

11. Another great chapter title was "Everybody Has One." If you remember the subject of that chapter, write the answer here:

12. Here's a tough one. What was the topic of the chapter called "Roses are Red"? Write the answer for that one here:

13. How about "Mood or 'Tude"? If you remember the subject of that chapter, then write the answer here:

14. Remember the chapter on symbolism? If we said Chi was like a tour guide who was as clever as a fox, that would be an example of what?

Write that answer here:

15. If we said that this book will call to you day after day, and it will call out to you until you pick it up and read it again, what kind of symbolism would that be? If you know the answer to this one, write the answer here:

16. Well, here's our last question for you. In the last chapter, we all felt the need, the need for what? Slowly, ever so slowly write the answer here:

Ok, that's it. We wish this moment could last forever and it makes us misty-eyed just thinking about how far you've come in the hours that we've spent together. You know, it *can* last forever if you never close this book!

Enough, already! Let's just leave with our pride at least a little intact!

You're right, Chi. Go outside and get some air. But in parting, we'd like to end our journey with some friendly advice to you:

Read,

read, and

read some more. We guarantee that you will discover the joy of reading and, while you're at it, you'll become a better reader. Until next time, dear readers, it's time to bounce.

Later!

Hold up! You forgot the answers, smart guy!

Oh, my bad. Here they are:

1. pencil, ruler, notebook, dictionary
2. italics, underlines, bolds
3. bread choice
4. sugar
5. ice cream

6. one hundred
7. Scooby Doo's
8. Shuckle
9. Bunko
10. predictions
11. opinions
12. literature
13. tone
14. simile
15. personification
16. speed

And if you can find those words (across, down, vertically, or backward) in the following word search, I have some advice for you.

Puzzle 5

O	N	E	I	D	M	E	C	R	E	A	M	K	P	B
Q	K	G	I	M	L	V	C	O	B	Z	S	A	U	P
L	D	L	O	K	N	U	B	I	Z	S	M	I	U	Z
P	E	R	S	O	N	I	F	I	C	A	T	I	O	N
W	C	A	V	S	N	L	W	C	O	J	Y	U	L	K
D	E	E	P	S	E	K	E	X	R	D	R	N	I	O
C	A	D	R	Y	B	O	O	C	S	C	A	D	T	O
U	Y	B	S	S	I	M	I	L	E	U	N	E	E	B
P	R	E	D	I	C	T	I	O	N	S	O	R	R	E
P	E	N	C	I	L	O	T	R	R	U	I	L	A	T
S	D	L	O	B	D	X	O	U	A	T	T	I	T	O
D	A	E	R	B	G	V	N	L	G	B	C	N	U	N
E	L	K	C	U	H	S	E	E	U	U	I	E	R	B
O	P	I	N	I	O	N	S	R	S	R	D	S	E	S
L	I	T	A	L	I	C	S	H	U	N	D	R	E	D

BOLDS
BREAD
BUNKO
CREAM
DICTIONARY
HUNDRED
ICE
ITALICS
LITERATURE
NOTEBOOK
ONE
OPINIONS
PENCIL
PERSONIFICATION
PREDICTIONS
RULER
SCOOBY
SHUCKLE
SIMILE
SPEED
SUGAR
TONE
UNDERLINES

Wise Note

Ok, here's the advice: Turn the page for the answers to the puzzles. You thought I had something *wise* to tell you? HA! Get real. I'm outta here.

See 'ya!

Puzzle Solutions

Puzzle 1

Puzzle 2

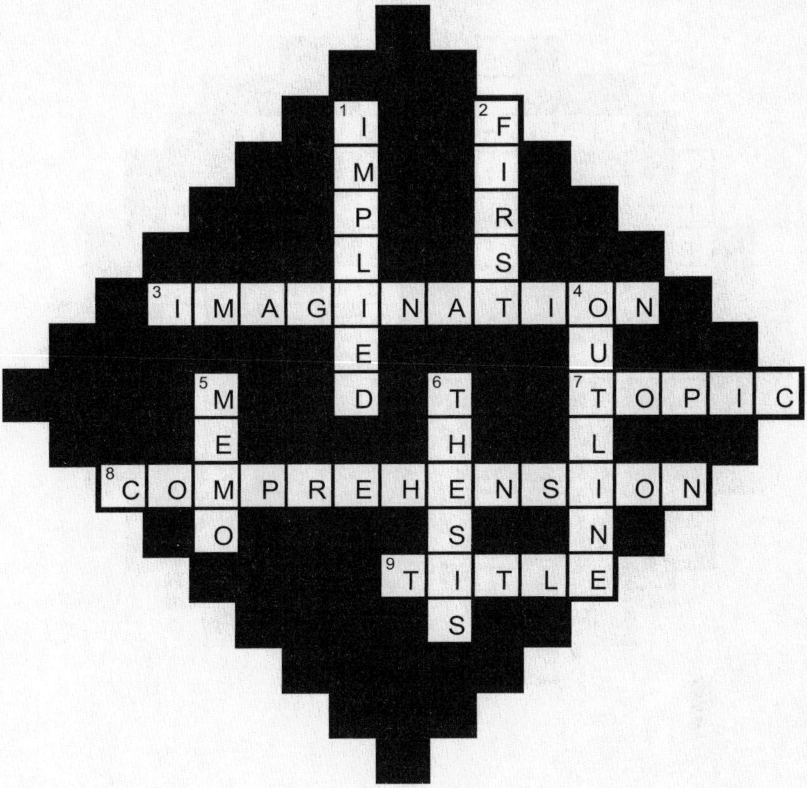

1 IMPLIED
2 FIRST
3 IMAGINATION
4 OUTLINE
5 MEMO
6 THESIS
7 TOPIC
8 COMPREHENSION
9 TITLE

Puzzle 3

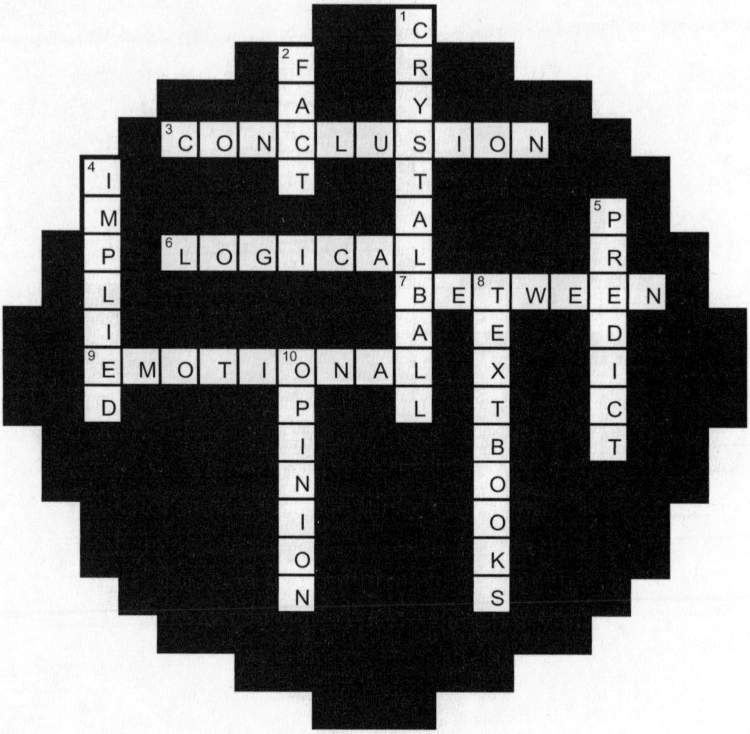
1 CRYSTALBALL
2 FACT
3 CONCLUSION
4 IMPLIED
5 PREDICT
6 LOGICAL
7 BETWEEN
8 TEXTBOOKS
9 EMOTIONAL
10 OPINION

Puzzle 4

1 P
2 POINT OF VIEW
3 THEME
4 PROSE
4 POETRY
5 SIMILE
6 LITERATURE
1 PERSONIFICATION
7 THIRD
8 FIRST
9 SECOND
10 TONE
11 METAPHOR
12 EPICS

Puzzle 5

O	N	E	I	D	M	E	C	R	E	A	M	K	P	B
Q	K	G	I	M	L	V	C	O	B	Z	S	A	U	P
L	D	L	O	K	N	U	B	I	Z	S	M	I	U	Z
P	E	R	S	O	N	I	F	I	C	A	T	I	O	N
W	C	A	V	S	N	L	W	C	O	J	Y	U	L	K
D	E	E	P	S	E	K	E	X	R	D	R	N	I	O
C	A	D	R	Y	B	O	O	C	S	C	A	D	T	O
U	Y	B	S	S	I	M	I	L	E	U	N	E	E	B
P	R	E	D	I	C	T	I	O	N	S	O	R	R	E
P	E	N	C	I	L	O	T	R	R	U	I	L	A	T
S	D	L	O	B	D	X	O	U	A	T	T	I	T	O
D	A	E	R	B	G	V	N	L	G	B	C	N	U	N
E	L	K	C	U	H	S	E	E	U	U	I	E	R	B
O	P	I	N	I	O	N	S	R	S	R	D	S	E	S
L	I	T	A	L	I	C	S	H	U	N	D	R	E	D

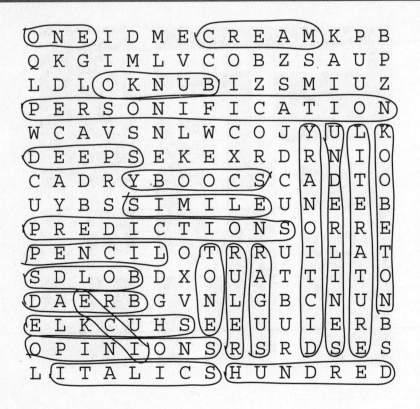

Just wanted to say, hi. No, really, the author needed to fill up some white space, so he asked me to sit here.

a
X
M
M